Interdepartmental Committee for Meteorological Services
and Supporting Research (ICMSSR)

Committee for Environmental Services, Operations and Research Needs (CESORN)

Working Group for Disaster Impact Assessments and Plans: Weather and Water Data
(WG/DIAP)

NATIONAL PLAN FOR DISASTER IMPACT ASSESSMENTS: WEATHER AND WATER DATA

Office of the Federal Coordinator for
Meteorological Services and Supporting Research

8455 Colesville Road, Suite 1500
Silver Spring, Maryland 20910
301-427-2002
www.ofcm.gov

FCM-P33-2010
Washington, DC
November 2010

FOREWORD

The *National Plan for Disaster Impact Assessments: Weather and Water Data* (NPDIA) describes collaborative mechanisms and procedures for coordinating disaster impact assessment and planning activities for significant storm events among participating Federal agencies and their affiliated partner organizations. This plan supersedes the *National Post-Storm Data Acquisition Plan* (March 2003).

The NPDIA represents the collaborative efforts of members of the Working Group for Disaster Impact Assessments and Plans: Weather and Water Data (WG/DIAP), which was previously named the Working Group for Natural Disaster Reduction and Post-Storm Data Acquisition. The WG/DIAP consists of representatives from applicable Federal agencies and partner organizations on items of mutual interest and concern related to the acquisition, dissemination, preservation, and exchange of perishable environmental data during and following a significant storm, flood, tornado, and/or tsunami event.

The intent of the NPDIA is to describe the types of data required or desired by the participating entities and the means these entities will use to coordinate data acquisition and data management activities. It is not the goal of this plan to prescribe the data acquisition activities of participating agencies, but instead to coordinate those activities already required by existing agency mission directives. The procedures outlined herein will likely be revised and refined as experience is gained from their application.

The effectiveness of this plan begins with the participation and cooperation of the agency representatives assigned as members of the working group, along with the participation of the group's affiliates. I want to personally thank everybody that contributed to the development of the NPDIA (see Appendix L). The results of the disaster impact assessment activities described in the NPDIA will enable better preparations for future disaster events and help mitigate their impacts.

//SIGNED//
Samuel P. Williamson
Federal Coordinator for Meteorological Services
 and Supporting Research

TABLE OF CONTENTS

Appendices

    A.   NPDIA Support for Emergency Support Functions

    B.   Agency/Entity Authority and Mission Statements

    C.   Links for Participating Federal Agencies and Entities

    D.   National Oceanic and Atmospheric Administration Internal Procedures

    E.   U.S Geological Survey Internal Procedures

    F.   Civil Air Patrol Forms

    G.   Pre-Scripted Mission Assignment

    H.   FEMA National Response Coordination Center Critical Phone Numbers

    I.   Data Access

    J.   Abbreviations and Acronyms

    K.   Examples of Past Disaster Impact Assessments

    L.   Working Group for Disaster Impact Assessments and Plans: Weather and Water Data

Tables

EXECUTIVE SUMMARY

The need for a national plan for disaster impact assessments stems from recognition by several Federal agencies that they were gathering complementary and, in some cases, overlapping and duplicate weather and water data for significant storm events. These agencies desired to improve the efficiency of their individual data collection efforts, leverage the efforts of others, and share these data through an organized, interagency disaster impact assessment process.

A series of informal meetings were held, data acquisition capabilities and requirements of the interested agencies were identified, and a number of recommendations resulted. The *National Plan for Disaster Impact Assessments: Weather and Water Data (NPDIA)* addresses the principal recommendations by documenting the types of data required, the acquisition processes, and the coordinating procedures to be used leading up to, during, and following a significant storm event. This national plan serves as a framework for both coordination of data acquisition activities of the participating agencies during a significant event and the documentation and deposition of data and products following that event. Funding for the activities of the participating agencies is provided primarily by the individual agency's parent organization or through the Department of Homeland Security in support of one or more of the Emergency Support Functions found in the National Response Framework.

The storm events addressed in this plan include land-falling tropical cyclones (hurricanes/typhoons and tropical storms), coastal extra-tropical storms (Nor'easters), severe convective outbreaks (tornadoes and windstorms), riverine and flash flooding, tsunamis, coastal and lake waves, and wind waves. The plan includes data requirements and acquisition capabilities of participating agencies, event response procedures and initiation criteria, coordination procedures, contact information, and data archival procedures. An agency response to a particular event is the responsibility of the individual agency according to its mission requirements, data needs, and available resources.

This plan is a dynamic document that will be reviewed annually. The contributors to its development anticipate and expect that the plan will evolve over time to reflect changes in the missions and resources of the participating agencies, the addition of types of hazards included in the plan, and the incorporation of evolving technologies.

As the body of data acquired and exchanged by the participating agencies grows, preparation of improved event and actuarial statistics becomes feasible. Responsibilities and methodologies for preparation of these statistics could become elements of future versions of this plan. Improved statistics on storm events should prove useful to private sector institutions such as insurance companies, as well as to Federal agencies.

INTRODUCTION

1.1   General

Disasters can be informative. When powerful storms and major floods damage or destroy our communities and infrastructure we can learn from the experience. That learning can lead to more accurate forecasts; better designed building, transportation, and communication systems; more robust response and recovery mechanisms; and more effective land use planning. But a key piece of such learning involves close technical observation and measurement of the factors that characterize the event and its impacts on communities, infrastructure, and environment. Making those observations and measurements during the event requires a timely and well-coordinated deployment of engineers, scientists, technicians, and equipment into affected areas. The *National Plan for Disaster Impact Assessments and Plans: Weather and Water Data (NPDIA)* establishes a procedural template that addresses this need.

The motivation for development of a national plan is threefold. The first motive is to minimize or eliminate the duplication of effort by agencies performing post-event data acquisition, thereby making the best use of the limited resources available to perform these surveys. The second is to assure these highly perishable data are indeed collected and that they are collected in conformance with the requirements (e.g., degree of accuracy) of all participating data users. It is generally acknowledged that the acquisition of these data is urgent; the physical effects that fully characterize a storm event are transient and can begin to change or be obliterated immediately after the event. The third motive is to define the coordination procedures of the agencies participating in the acquisition of storm event environmental data and to collaborate on data sharing and on ensuring that means for data archival and future retrieval are established.

1.2   Scope

The procedures outlined herein apply to the conterminous 48 states, Alaska, Hawaii, the Commonwealth of Puerto Rico, and the Virgin Islands, Guam, American Samoa, and the Confederation of Northern Marianna Islands. This plan defines the roles and coordinating procedures of the agencies participating in the acquisition of storm event environmental data. When only a single agency is involved in a storm event response, that agency should follow procedures specified in its internal documents, but those practices should be consistent with those contained herein. It is recognized that many Federal missions are undertaken in the overall response and recovery process that follows a significant storm event. The intent of this plan is to address an important, though limited, aspect of this response process.

Environmental events addressed in this plan include land-falling tropical cyclones (hurricanes/typhoons and tropical storms), dangerous coastal extra-tropical storms, severe convective outbreaks (tornadoes and windstorms), riverine and flash flooding, and tsunamis. The plan includes data requirements and acquisition capabilities of the participating agencies, event response initiation criteria, coordination procedures, agency points of contact, and data deposition procedures.

While the 2003 *National Post-Storm Data Acquisition Plan*, which the NPDIA supersedes, addressed post-storm activities, new technologies have ushered in opportunities to pre-deploy, increase the density of, and harden observation systems, thereby providing the capability to collect and disseminate real-time data of relevance to those who forecast the events and manage Federal, State, and local response and recovery. These data support those agencies that characterize the actual event to improve scientific understanding and modeling capabilities. With the addition of real-time data, this new NPDIA supports nearly all of the Emergency Support Functions (ESFs) in the National Response Framework in either a real-time or long-term application. ESFs and descriptions of the support provided to the ESFs by the NPDIA are listed in Appendix A.

1.3   Goals

The following goals of the NPDIA expand upon the objectives contained in the Terms of Reference for the Working Group for Disaster Impact Assessments and Plans: Weather and Water Data (WG/DIAP):

- Identifying the requirements, resources, and capabilities of the participating agencies
- Developing procedures for coordinating agency activities during and following storm events
- Developing mechanisms for aggregating and sharing resources among the participating agencies
- Preparing summaries of event documentation and data acquired under this national plan

As experience is gained in responding to events and procedures become more refined and efficient, resources available outside the participating agencies should be identified and arrangements made to access these resources. Examples of such resources include aircraft for transport of personnel and for aerial photoreconnaissance, expertise residing in academic institutions for field assessment and interpretation of storm effects and damage, and data acquired during scientific field experiments involving the same or similar storm events.

1.4   Participating Federal Agencies

The Office of the Federal Coordinator for Meteorological Services and Supporting Research (OFCM). The OFCM facilitates Federal agency coordination for storm event assessments and plans and assumes overall responsibility for the preparation and maintenance of the NPDIA. The role each agency assumes during a storm event period is determined by the individual agency's authority and mission requirements. Appendix B contains authority and mission statements of individual agencies and entities referenced in the NPDIA.

1.4.1 Department of Agriculture (USDA)

Natural Resources Conservation Service (NRCS). The NRCS leads the Federal commitment to the conservation of all natural resources by ensuring private lands are conserved, restored, and more resilient to environmental challenges, including climate change. The NRCS works with landowners through conservation planning and assistance designed to benefit the soil, water, air, plants, and animals that result in productive lands and healthy ecosystems. The NRCS provides technical and financial assistance through local conservation districts to land users, communities, watershed groups, Federal and State agencies, American Indian tribes, and others at their request. At the local level, the NRCS staff works alongside State and local conservation staff and volunteers in a partnership to care for natural resources on private lands. The NRCS develops comprehensive technical guidance for conservation planning and assistance.

1.4.2 Department of Commerce (DOC)

National Oceanic and Atmospheric Administration (NOAA)

Within the DOC, NOAA is the principal meteorological agency of the Federal government. By law, NOAA is responsible for reporting the weather of the United States, providing weather and flood warnings and forecasts to the general public, developing and furnishing applied weather services, and recording the climate of the United States. This mission is carried out within NOAA by the National Weather Service (NWS); National Environmental Satellite, Data, and Information Service (NESDIS); Office of Oceanic and Atmospheric Research (OAR); National Ocean Service (NOS); and NOAA Marine and Aviation Operations (NMAO).

NWS. The NWS consists of a national headquarters in Silver Spring, Maryland; 6 regional headquarters across the continental United States, Alaska, and the Pacific; 122 Weather Forecast Offices (WFOs); and 13 River Forecast Centers. The River Forecast Centers provide basin-specific forecast guidance on riverine and flash flooding. The NWS has two Tsunami Warning Centers that provide reliable tsunami detection, forecasts, and warnings in the United States. In addition, the NWS's National Centers for Environmental Prediction (NCEP) include the following service centers: Environmental Modeling Center, Storm Prediction Center (SPC), NCEP Central Operations, Hydrometeorological Prediction Center, Ocean Prediction Center, Tropical Prediction Center, Climate Prediction Center, Aviation Weather Center, and Space Environment Center. These service centers provide the expertise to produce focused guidance, modeling, and numerical weather prediction for severe local storms, marine weather, tropical weather, climatic trends, aviation weather, and the space environment. This support provides basic information for both the NWS WFOs and external users, including other Federal agencies and Federal, State, and local emergency management officials. Respondents in the event of tornadoes and other severe convective storms, flooding, and other weather-related natural disasters, represent all strata of the NWS, depending on the type of event. Warning Coordination Meteorologists (WCM) at each of the WFOs are often the initial NWS responders to all major weather events, documenting apparent damage and causal effects, as well as gathering commentary from witnesses.

NOS. The NOS provides science-based solutions through collaborative partnerships to address evolving economic, environmental, and social pressures on our oceans and coasts. This effort includes protecting coastal communities; monitoring our oceans and coasts; promoting safe, efficient and environmentally sound marine transportation; reducing ocean and coastal health risks; and protecting coastal and marine places. The NOS has eight program offices and two staff offices that manage and preserve the Nation's ocean and coasts.

Coastal Services Center (CSC). The CSC supports the environmental, social, and economic well being of the coast by linking people, information, and technology. It helps communities prepare for and respond to coastal hazards. The Center's coastal hazards toolkit of services for State and local organizations allows users to quickly find the hazard-related information they need, effectively apply it, and visually showcase the results to their constituents and other end users. The coastal hazards toolkit of services provides data and information, data analysis, and visualization tools. These products and services help coastal regions prepare for and react to both chronic episodic events and longer-term climate change issues such as sea-level rise.

Center for Operational Oceanographic Products and Services (CO-OPS). The CO-OPS collects and distributes observations and predictions of water levels and currents to ensure safe, efficient, and environmentally sound maritime commerce. It provides the set of water level and coastal current products required to support NOS's Strategic Plan mission requirements and to assist in providing operational oceanographic data and products required by NOAA's other Strategic Plan themes. The CO-OPS manages the National Water Level Observation Network (NWLON), and a national network of Physical Oceanographic Real-Time Systems (PORTS) in major U.S. harbors. It establishes standards for the collection and processing of water level and current data, collects and documents user requirements that serve as the foundation for all resulting program activities, designs new and/or improved oceanographic observing systems, designs software to improve its data processing capabilities, maintains and operates oceanographic observing systems, performs operational data analysis and quality control, and produces and disseminates oceanographic products.

Office of Response and Restoration (OR&R). The OR&R protects coastal and marine resources, mitigates threats, reduces harm, and restores ecological function. It provides comprehensive solutions to environmental hazards caused by oil, chemicals, and marine debris. To fulfill its mission of protecting and restoring NOAA trust resources, the OR&R provides scientific and technical support to prepare for and respond to oil and chemical releases, determines damage to natural resources from these releases, protects and restores marine and coastal ecosystems including coral reefs, and works with communities to address critical local and regional coastal challenges

National Geodetic Survey (NGS). The NGS and its predecessor agencies have been world leaders in geodesy and cartography, with a focus on enabling safe and efficient transportation. For decades the NGS has collected remotely sensed aerial data to support two primary programs:

the Coastal Mapping Program (CMP) and Aeronautical Survey Program (ASP). The CMP delivers accurate and up-to-date National Shoreline maps. In addition to promoting safe marine navigation, the National Shoreline provides the basis for a multitude of legal boundaries. The ASP delivers airport obstruction charts and other products used to design and validate the instrument approaches required for aircraft to land at U.S. airports during inclement weather. Through the capability to execute these programs, NGS provides emergency response imagery in the wake of national disasters.

National Institute of Standards and Technology (NIST)

NIST promotes U.S. innovation and competitiveness by anticipating and meeting the measurement science, standards, and technology needs of the U.S. building and fire safety industries in ways that enhance economic security and improve the quality of life. Through its Materials and Construction Research Division, NIST conducts laboratory, field, and analytical research in structural engineering, including the investigation of important structural failures, the characterization of building loads during construction and during their service life, and structural response analyses. Extreme events, such as hurricanes and tornadoes, are viewed as opportunities to evaluate the performance of structures subjected to wind loads that may approach or exceed the ultimate limit states of the structure. Beginning with Hurricane Camille in 1969, the Structures Division has conducted post-storm assessments on its own or in collaboration with other Federal agencies, universities, and building research centers.

1.4.3 Department of Defense (DOD)

U.S. Army Corps of Engineers (USACE) and U.S. Air Force (USAF), Civil Air Patrol (CAP)-USAF Auxiliary. The DOD is represented by elements of the U.S. Army and USAF, primarily by the USACE and the Civil Air Patrol (CAP), a civilian auxiliary of the USAF. The USACE has primary responsibility for construction and maintenance of marine navigation in public waterways and for coastal storm protection projects on public lands. USACE post-event activities are coordinated through the Office of Chief of Engineers, and the Engineer Research and Development Center (ERDC). The CAP and the Air Force Reserve Command's 53rd Weather Reconnaissance Squadron (53 WRS) serve principally in a supporting role to the other participating agencies.

1.4.4 Department of Homeland Security (DHS)

Federal Emergency Management Agency (FEMA). The DHS and FEMA within it are the Federal coordinating agencies that respond to major disasters or threats in the United States and its territories. FEMA provides response and recovery and hazard mitigation assistance, emergency management preparedness training, flood insurance, and funding for related studies and services. Headquartered in Washington, DC, FEMA has 10 regional offices, with field offices and special facilities located nationwide. The National Response Coordination Center (NRCC), located in Washington DC, assists in coordinating efforts among all Federal office. ESF Coordinator positions within the NRCC are activated for exercises and emergencies.

1.4.5 Department of the Interior (DOI)

U.S. Geological Survey (USGS). USGS is the principal Earth science agency responsible for collection, assessment, and dissemination of information regarding the geology, topography, mineral resources, hydrology, and biology of the United States. USGS is a nationally recognized provider of water data and information for use by others to design, operate, manage, and regulate water resources; establish floodplain boundaries; issue flood warnings and river forecasts; and manage emergency operations. Its real-time and long-term flow records and stage-discharge relationships (ratings) are key inputs for NWS forecast models. USGS peak-flow data are fundamental to flood-frequency analyses, on which the design of dams and the delineation of flood-insurance rate maps depend.

1.4.6 Department of Transportation (DOT)

Federal Highway Administration (FHWA). The FHWA, though not an active NPDIA participant, is expected to become more involved in the future. While the agency has no requirements to acquire environmental data following significant storm events, it works with State and local departments of transportation, which are building sites capable of acquiring and disseminating storm event data. These sites, which monitor the highway system, could eventually be used in the coordinated storm event data acquisition process under the NPDIA.

1.5   Affiliated Organizations

The following entities have participated in the WG/DIAP and are active partners in the acquisition and assessment of storm event environmental data under the NPDIA.

1.5.1 The American Association for Wind Engineering (AAWE)

The AAWE is a consortium of wind and surge experts affiliated with research universities, industry, and private consulting. These experts collaborate to collect field data before, during, and after U.S. land-falling hurricanes; promote and investigate effective mitigation; and contribute to the development of national codes and standards for wind resistant design. The AAWE is a national, nonprofit, technical society of engineers, meteorologists, architects, planners, public officials, social scientists, manufacturers and constructors. Included among AAWE members are researchers, practicing professionals, educators, government officials, and building code regulators.

1.5.2 Coasts, Oceans, Ports and Rivers Institute (COPRI)

COPRI is one of eight institutes under the American Society of Civil Engineering. It supports and advances specific civil engineering specialties focused on the technical, educational, scientific, and professional issues unique to coastal, ocean, port, waterway, wetland, and riverine environments. COPRI strives to advance and disseminate scientific and engineering knowledge relevant to its diverse membership.

1.5.3 The Digital Hurricane Consortium (DHC)

The DHC consists of faculty from participating universities, the Center for Severe Weather Research (CSWR), and the Applied Technology Council (ATC). This consortium was formed to better respond to severe weather events, especially hurricanes, by mobilizing field deployed equipment to collect wind field and storm surge measurements that are extremely useful in determining not only the strength of the event but how the built environment responded to the event in terms of damage. Members of the consortium are also active in the AAWE. Participating faculty come from universities across the country, including Clemson University, Colorado University, Florida International University, Louisiana State University, Oklahoma University, Texas Tech University (TTU), University of Alabama at Huntsville, University of Florida, and University of Notre Dame.

1.6   The WG/DIAP

Appendix. L lists, by name and organization, the WG/DIAP members from Federal agencies and the participants from affiliated organizations who collaborated on this edition of the NPDIA. Appendix C provides Internet links to participating agency/entity home pages (most of which contain organization charts). Contact information (telephone numbers and email addresses) for all members and participants is located on the WG/DIAP web page: http://www.ofcm.gov/wg-diap/index.htm.

OPERATIONS AND PROCEDURES

2.1 General

An agency response to an event deemed to be under this plan shall be at the discretion and within the mission authority and resources of that agency. The OFCM serves as the executive agent to coordinate multiple agency responses. The agencies participating in this effort typically have overlapping requirements for the event responses and data types. Agencies often acquire the same data type following an event but may use the data for substantially different purposes. For example, inundation data following a coastal storm may be used by one agency for flood hazard risk assessment purposes while another agency may use the same data for structural performance evaluation purposes. There may be events where some agencies have little or no interest and no mission authority. An example would be a severe tornado outbreak. Unless the event directly affected a DOD installation, the DOD probably would have no justification for a response within the scope of this plan.

2.2 Intent

The plan of operations described herein is formulated to ensure that agency responses to mutually examined events are adequate, while minimizing the expenditure of resources on events of interest to a single agency or events of no common interest. Moreover, the plan has been organized to allow for changes in the scope of responses to particular types of events and for adoption or implementation of emerging technology, without requiring a revision of the entire plan.

2.3 Activation Criteria

Activation criteria for initiating agency responses to a particular event depend upon the event. Events for which there is typically adequate warning such as land-falling storms and inland floods permit evaluation of the situation as it develops. For other events, such as tsunamis and tornadoes, there may be little or no warning and little time to assess the initial effects of the event. A timely response therefore requires that activation criteria be based upon the presumption of occurrence of a significant event. Table 2.1 shows most of the common activation criteria that would initiate a team or individual-agency effort. Links to the Saffir-Simpson and Enhanced Fujita (EF) scales are as follows:

- Saffir-Simpson Hurricane Wind Scale: http://www.nhc.noaa.gov/aboutsshws.shtml

- Enhanced Fujita Tornado Intensity Scale: http://www.spc.noaa.gov/efscale/ef-scale.html

Table 2.1 Event Activation Criteria
5-Day tropical forecast indicates land-falling hurricane
NWS Deployment of a Quick Response Team (QRT) (see section 2.4.3 and appendix D)
An unusually high surge (in an historical context) at a particular coastal location
An unusually prolonged period (e.g., several days) of elevated coastal water levels
An extended reach (hundreds of miles) of affected coastline
Prolonged and/or unusually high surface wind speeds
Unusually long (> 16s) wind-generated wave periods along the Atlantic and Gulf of Mexico coasts
Precipitation rates resulting in total rainfall that could cause potential flooding or flash-flooding
Freezing and/or precipitation to the extent that accumulation of snow/ice on roadways, railways, airports, or walkways is expected to cause such modes of transportation to become inoperative
Accumulation of snow/ice on the built environment is expected to become a hazard due to structural failure
Severe convective wind damage
Tornado outbreak
Tsunami reported
Tsunami warning issued based on seismic data of sub-sea earthquake
Ice jamming
Dam or levee failure or potential failure
Flash floods

2.4   Collaboration and Communications

2.4.1   Disaster Event Notification and Response Coordination Procedures

2.4.1.a Notification. The first member to recognize or foresee a significant event and identify the need for a coordinated disaster impact assessment should alert the rest of the team. The alert notification mechanism for all event types is by group email: diap.alerts@noaa.gov. The initial alert email may be sent by any member. The group email account includes all WG/DIAP members and will automatically disseminate the alert email to them. The initial email should contain a brief description of the event, the source of the event information, any planned data collection and timelines, and a proposed date/time for the first response coordination teleconference. Depending on the urgency and lead time, the initiator may need to follow up with phone calls to key team members. The member list with contact information is located on the WG/DIAP web site http://www.ofcm.gov/wg-diap/index.htm and is maintained by OFCM. Follow-up email replies may be sent by any member. *(Note: to reply to all members when replying to group emails, the group email address must be added as an addressee).*

2.4.1.b Response Coordination Teleconferences. Response coordination teleconferences will be initiated by OFCM or any lead agency. They will be convened as needed prior to, during, and after response activities to discuss and coordinate response activities. These may be supplemented by web-based capabilities such as GoToMeeting and Chat services. Teleconference, GoToMeeting, and Chat services may be initiated by OFCM or any member agency having these or similar capabilities.

2.4.1.c AAWE Unique Procedures for Tornado Response. For tornadoes suspected by the National Weather Service (NWS) of producing greater than EF3 damage, a Quick Response Team (QRT) may be dispatched by the NWS. NWS Headquarters, Office of Climate, Water, and Weather Services (OCWWS), will notify OFCM of the QRT deployment. OFCM will then alert AAWE and all appropriate members of the WG/DIAP about the deployment and initiate coordination between AAWE and the NWS for collaborative disaster impact assessment actions.

2.4.2 Response Procedures

Coordination of agency responses to an event is desired when there are common activities in a common geographic area and common or overlapping data requirements. The specific agency actions in response to an event will depend to some extent on the nature and characteristics of the event. Table 2.2 lists some of the basic response procedures leading up to, during, and after an event. The choice of responses will vary from event to event.

Table 2.2 Response Procedures	Tropical	Extra-tropical	Severe convective	Tsunamis	Riverine flooding
Event – 5 Days					
USGS: Run Hurricane Response Plan (see appendix E)	X				
Event – 3 Days					
NOAA National Geodetic Survey: Consider/coordinate pre-storm baseline flights leading up to event. (See NOAA/NGS internal plans at appendix D.)	X				X
DHC: Coordinate sensor placement with other team members.	X				
USGS, USACE, FEMA, NOAA: Formulate coordinated effort for high-water mark sensor placement plan	X	X			X
NOAA CSC: Provide mapping support where needed to FEMA for decision briefings using NWS data in GIS formats. Have been based on mission assignments in the past. Tutorial could be used to train FEMA and NOAA staff: http://www.csc noaa.gov/storm_info/tutorial html	X				X
NIST, NOAA, AAWE, and DHC: Begin plan for pre-event sensor placement and post-event assessment of structural damage.	X	X			X
Event + 0 Days					
All Agencies: Secure lodging near enough to affected area to deploy quickly but far enough away to be safe.	X	X	X	X	X
NOAA National Geodetic Survey: Plan post-storm data collection flights after event. (See NOAA/NGS internal plans at appendix D.)	X	X	X	X	X
Event + 1 Day					
All Agencies (usually NWS Regional Offices): Request CAP post-event over flight to capture photographs of damage, flooding extent, dam/levee condition etc.	X	X	X	X	X
NWS: If tornado is estimated at EF-3 or stronger, a Quick Response Team may be deployed. (See section 2.4.3 and NOAA internal plans at appendix D.)			X		

Table 2.2 Response Procedures	Tropical	Extra-tropical	Severe convective	Tsunamis	Riverine flooding
USDA: Provide data on precipitation effects.	X	X	X		X
NIST, NOAA, AAWE, and DHC: Coordinate field evaluation of structural performance if event warrants.	X	X	X	X	X
NWS: Consider deploying Survey Teams and notify other members.				X	X
NWS: Consider deploying Quick Response Team and notify other members.	X	X	X	X	X
NOAA Office of Coast Survey: Consider post-storm hydrographic surveys (as needed to clear waterways and re-open ports) and notify other members	X				
USACE, USGS, FEMA, and NWS: Collaborate on high-priority sites for flood data collection.					X
USGS, USACE: For riverine flooding, coordinate collection of hydrologic data and discharge rates.					X
Event + 3 Days					
USGS, USACE, and FEMA: Deploy teams to collect high-water marks no later than event + 72 hours if possible.	X				X

2.4.3 NWS Quick Response Team

For tornadoes suspected of producing greater than EF3 damage, a special Quick Response Team (QRT) may be dispatched by the NWS. NWS policy for disaster impact assessments, including QRTs, is located at: http://www.nws.noaa.gov/directives/sym/pd01016004curr.pdf. The NWS QRT enlists experienced wind damage expert(s) to determine the final EF scale rating for these events. These experts include but are not limited to members of the AAWE, other NWS personnel, members of the academic community, and other private sector wind damage experts. They possess expertise in the areas of wind and associated wind-driven water loads on buildings and structures; societal impacts of winds, hurricanes and tornadoes; risk assessment; cost-benefit analysis; codes and standards; dispersion of urban and industrial pollution; wind energy; urban aerodynamics; etc.

2.4.4. Civil Air Patrol Aerial Survey Support Requests

To request CAP missions to assess storm damage events, the requester (e.g., a NWS regional headquarters or WFO) fills out a request form, which is available online at: https://ocwws.weather.gov/intranet/psda/psda.php. This site is maintained by NOAA/NWS, Chris Maier, 301-713-0090 x 175, NWS/CAP point of contact. During OFCM office hours, the requester sends the request to the OFCM CAP group email address: nws.ofcm.cap@noaa.gov (shown on the request form in Appendix F). This group email list includes the primary OFCM mission approval point of contact (WG/DIAP Executive Secretary)

2.5 Data Acquisition Procedures

Because all events covered in this plan share some common characteristics, the data acquisition procedures share some similarities. Table 2.3 provides general guidance on procedures, type, and quantity of data. Appendix E contains an example of detailed procedures to be used for high-water mark identification and recovery used by USGS.

Table 2.3 Data Acquisition Procedures	Tropical	Extra-tropical	Severe convective	Tsunamis	Riverine flooding
ALL Agencies: For Federal, State, local, and tribal situational awareness, identify your personnel working in the field.	X	X	X	X	X
DHC: Coordinate with participating agencies for potential data collections locations.	X				
DHC: (Real-Time Collectors) Collect and provide real-time wind speed, wind direction, temperature, humidity, and barometric pressure data from multiple monitoring assets to the NWS and to the Hurricane Research Division of NOAA/OAR.					
NOAA NOS: Collect and provide real-time water level and meteorological data from coastal tide gauges to NWS and via the web.	X	X	X	X	
DHC: (Non-Real-Time Collectors) Collect other non-real-time assets after it is safe to enter the collections areas and disseminate the data.	X				
USGS, USACE, AAWE, NIST, DHC : Collect hydrodynamic and structural effects data and available hydrographs acquired at open ocean and affected coastal locations. Estimates of the net sub-sea bottom displacement are desirable.	X			X	X
AAWE: Coordinate with federal agencies to provide post-storm damage assessments as needed.	X	X	X	X	X
USGS, FEMA, NWS, and NIST: Form agency high-water mark collections teams and coordinate collections between agencies.	X	X	X	X	X
USDA: Provide available precipitation, soil erosion, and agricultural damage data.	X			X	X
NIST, NOAA: Provide field teams to assess the storm-induced structural damage. Where possible, prepare charts depicting estimates of the surface wind speeds inferred from structural effects.	X	X	X	X	X
NWS: Assemble and analyze damage survey findings, satellite and radar imagery, videotapes, and other information while determining the structure and organization of the tornadic storm(s).			X		
NWS: Perform post-event surveys documenting maximum inundation and societal impacts (effectiveness of the warning system and mitigation measures).				X	
NWS: Coordinate potential flooding areas with FEMA, USACE, and USGS.					X
NWS: Perform post-storm surveys documenting extreme conditions that led to flooding (precipitation and stream flow).					X

Table 2.3 Data Acquisition Procedures	Tropical	Extra-tropical	Severe convective	Tsunamis	Riverine flooding
USGS, USACE: Take discharge and current velocity measurements.					X
All Agencies: Store all information about each event.	X	X	X	X	X
OFCM: After most event actions and data collections are complete, build an event summary in accordance with guidance in chapter 4.	X	X	X	X	X

2.6   Data Repository and Retrieval

The data collected by each agency should be stored and backed up by the agency that collects the data. Appendix I includes agency-specific Internet links to access the collected data or other instructions for how to access the data. Additional data access information will be maintained on the WG/DIAP web site: http://www.ofcm.gov/wg-diap/index.htm. Metadata, information from each agency about the data types they collect, a description of the data quality for each data type, and pointers to the location of storage for the data should also be included. For all designated storm events, descriptions of current and ongoing response efforts (but not the actual data) will be stored for reference. After sufficient collection efforts have been completed for a given event, OFCM will collect all descriptive event files and consolidate them into an event summary (see chapter 4).

2.7   Funding

2.7.a Funding prior to a Federal Disaster Declaration. Leading up to an event, and before the President has declared the area a Federal disaster, funding for disaster impact assessment activities will be more difficult to obtain. FEMA uses a document called a Pre-Scripted Mission Assignment (PSMA), which allows funding for actions before declaration of disaster. During national emergencies, FEMA Federal Coordinating Officers (FCOs) must make a large number of important operations decisions in a short time under stressful conditions. The PSMAs aid the FCO by providing a prepackaged set of actions that can be executed easily and quickly. PSMAs must be validated at FEMA long before a disaster strikes to simplify the tasking and funding process. By instruction, only those actions that prevent loss of life or property can be funded by a PSMA. PSMAs may be a potential funding source for disaster impact assessment data collection activities. Appendix G includes an example of a PSMA form, as well as a NPDIA statement of work.

2.7.b Funding after a Federal Disaster Declaration. After the President declares an event location a Federal disaster area, FEMA can more readily release funding using Inter-Agency Agreements (IAAs). IAAs are contract agreements between two Federal agencies to exchange fees for a service. All participating agencies should consider building IAAs with DHS/FEMA to help facilitate funding. IAAs should be drafted, approved, and signed long before any disaster event requiring them.

2.7.c Agency Funding. For many smaller disaster events, it will be up to individual agencies to fund their disaster impact assessment activities. For example, the NWS funds the QRT in response to a tornado event. For some unusual riverine events, USGS will fund special sensing missions. For some agencies, such as NOAA, the funding for any operation must be available at the agency before work begins. This is true even if it is fairly certain that the operation will be funded at a later date from outside the agency.

2.7.d Civil Air Patrol Aerial Survey Support Funding. A five-year umbrella agreement among NWS, OFCM, and USAF is the funding vehicle for CAP missions to assess storm damage events for NWS units. (Limited funding may also be made available for other WG/DIAP participants.) Annual agreements under the five-year umbrella agreement provide funding for each fiscal year through OFCM.

CAPABILITIES AND REQUIREMENTS

3.1 USDA/NRCS Capabilities

The Rural Development Act of 1972, Public Law 92-419, Sec. 302, Title III (7 USC 1010a), August 30, 1972, authorized a land inventory and monitoring program, including studies and surveys of erosion, sediment damage, flood plain identification, and land-use changes and trends. The NRCS informs the USDA of the extent of short-duration natural phenomena that affect health, safety, and agricultural production. Reports document impacts of NRCS activities on resources and describe the event in quantitative terms, including amount of precipitation and surface-wind speeds.

The Watershed Protection and Flood Prevention Act (Public Law 83-566, Statute 606) authorizes the Secretary of Agriculture to cooperate with state and local governments in planning and conducting improvements for soil conservation and other purposes. The NRCS can prepare reports on the impact of serious storms on the installed project measures.

The Snow Survey and Water Supply Forecasting Program, administered by NRCS, is found in the Code of Federal Regulations: 7 CFR 612. NRCS is charged with the collection of snow data to develop monthly water supply forecasts from January through June in partnership with the NWS and with maintaining the data in a database and making it publically available. In partnership with other Federal, State, tribal, and local government agencies and utility companies, data are collected through a network of over 1,200 manual snow courses (measured monthly) and 752 automated SNOw TELemtry (SNOTEL) stations located throughout Alaska, Arizona, California, Colorado, Idaho, Montana, Nevada, New Mexico, Oregon, Utah, Washington, and Wyoming. SNOTEL stations located at high elevations throughout the mountainous west collect data year round on air temperature, precipitation, barometric pressure, wind speed and direction, relative humidity, snow depth, and snow water equivalent. This network is the only high elevation climate data collection network in the United States.

NRCS also operates the 150-station Soil Climate Analysis Network (SCAN). Automated SCAN stations are scattered across the United States and are located primarily on agricultural lands. These stations collect soil moisture and temperature data in addition to air temperature, precipitation, barometric pressure, wind speed and direction, relative humidity, solar radiation, and if appropriate, snow depth and snow water equivalent.

3.2　Department of Commerce Capabilities

3.2.1　NOAA Capabilities

NWS provides a continuous weather watch throughout the Americas and the Pacific, with lesser amounts of data collected globally. Data are gathered via remote sensing (e.g., satellite-based instruments, weather radar, and vertical sounders) as well as from in situ sensing (e.g., surface observations). Observational and computational information is processed through computer-based models to produce numerical weather prediction and river forecast products, which are available to users globally.

NOS capabilities include the following:

- NOS provides products, services, and data. Examples include nautical charts, a framework for consistent geographic reference, and tidal and water-level monitoring

- NOS manages 14 national marine sanctuaries and one national monument and provides funding to coastal states to manage 27 national estuarine research reserves

- NOS participates in immediate response to hazardous spill events, damage assessment, and restoration activities

- NOS supports states in protecting resources and guiding economic development in coastal areas. NOS also supports training for state coastal managers participating in the program.

- NOS assesses, monitors, and predicts the consequences of natural and human-induced environmental hazards such as hurricanes, erosion, and sea-level rise.

CSC provides training modules on how to access, process, and use NOAA forecast and observation data in geospatial formats before, during, and after a storm. The primary audience for the training modules includes DHS/FEMA personnel, NOAA Incident Coordination Center (ICC) staff, and NOAA Homeland Security Operations Center (HSOC) staff for creation of situational awareness maps for decision briefings.

Other CSC capabilities include the following:

- Provides natural hazard vulnerability analysis and assistance on coastal zone management and building community resilience

- Supplies geospatial technology (e.g., geographic information system [GIS]) assistance and coastal inundation information, supports application of GIS and remote sensing data

- Performs ecosystem and damage assessments

- Provides technical assistance in recovering fisheries, restoring habitat, and rebuilding coastal communities

- Provides technical assistance for disaster response, recovery, and rebuilding efforts to include coastal resource management

- Planning process support (includes community participation process design and facilitation) and assistance with recovery project development

CO-OPS provides real-time water levels, currents, winds, and other oceanographic and meteorological measurements for major U.S. port areas. This infrastructure acquires and disseminates observations and predictions necessary to ensure secure, safe, efficient, and environmentally sound maritime commerce. The real-time tides information and current critical infrastructure support national security, safe navigation, sustainable coastal communities, and disaster response. Real-time water levels and current information are essential to post-incident environmental impacts and waterway evacuation.

OR&R responds to and mitigates the consequences of spills and other hazards that threaten coastal environments. It provides accurate, timely, and relevant scientific advice to organizations charged with responding to and mitigating the consequences of spills and other hazards that threaten coastal environments and communities. The hazardous materials (HAZMAT) scientific team provides key technical advice during spills of oil or hazardous materials in the coastal zone. To do this, the HAZMAT team is on call 24 hours a day, every day of the year. The HAZMAT team also responds to other technological and natural coastal hazards such as hurricanes and airplane crashes. HAZMAT carries out these functions under the National Response Plan and the National Oil and Hazardous Substances Pollution Contingency Plan. This group operates CAMEO (Computer Aided Management to Emergency Operations), a well-known NOAA software program that is in use at over 10,000 locations. CAMEO provides first responders and emergency planners with information to respond quickly to chemical accidents. OR&R provides on-scene Scientific Support Coordinators and supporting field teams and reach-back technical support and scientific guidance to assist in response and restoration efforts.

NGS. Through its CMP and ASP, NGS utilizes both contracted and in-house assets to conduct end-to-end aerial surveys. NGS collects near-infrared and color (red, green, blue; RGB) imagery at a nominal one-foot ground sample distance (GSD). In conjunction with the NMAO Aircraft Operations Center (AOC), NOAA dedicates one specially modified turbojet aircraft to the NGS CMP and ASP and has several other aircraft that can be used on an as-needed basis. NGS's current emergency response workflow enables imagery to be processed and available via the Internet within 12 hours of collection. The speed with which NOAA can respond to an event depends upon several factors, the least controllable of which is weather. The imagery provided include individual ortho-rectified RGB images in JPEG format. The resulting GSD after ortho-rectification is 0.5 m. Delivery of the full-resolution TIFF images is not feasible via the Worldwide Web due to bandwidth limitations, as individual images in TIFF format are over 150 MB each. Special requests for these products are addressed on a case-by-case basis.

3.2.2 NIST Capabilities

A well-equipped structural testing laboratory and computer facilities for modeling loads and structural response are maintained by the Materials and Construction Research Division of NIST. The division's capabilities for predicting and assessing wind effects on buildings and other structures include computer codes for the simulation of extreme wind speeds in atmospheric boundary layers. The division also maintains special equipment and supplies needed for the rapid deployment of investigative teams following major wind and earthquake disasters, structural collapses, and building fires.

The Process Measurement Division of the Chemical Science and Technology Laboratory within NIST maintains wind and water tunnels for fluid mechanics research. Of particular interest is the closed-return, low-speed, low-turbulence wind tunnel facility, which serves as the U.S. primary standard for anemometer calibration. Interchangeable test sections allow calibrations at wind speeds of up to 67 ms^{-1} (149.87 mph). State-of-the-art flow visualization techniques, hot-wire anemometry, and laser-Doppler velocimetry are available in this laboratory.

3.3   DOD Capabilities

3.3.1 USACE

The ERDC, in cooperation with participating USACE district offices, can provide data on near-shore wave conditions, winds, and water levels; beach profiles; lidar topographic and bathymetric surveys; aerial photography/imagery; damage assessment to marinas, coastal projects and navigation channels and structures; morphological changes to beaches; and identification of high-water marks.

The Joint Airborne Lidar Bathymetry Technical Center of Expertise executes the USACE National Coastal Mapping Program (NCMP), which provides lidar elevation and imagery data to support regional and scale management activities. The data are collected with a unique in-house survey capability that collects lidar topographic elevations and lidar water depths, both with concurrent digital aerial photography and hyperspectral imagery, for land use and habitat characterization. This capability was used in the aftermath of the 2004 and 2005 hurricane seasons to provide elevation and imagery data for more than 2,000 miles of shoreline, in addition to the 3,500 miles collected as part of the NCMP since 2004.

NCMP data support the quantification of economic, environmental, and engineering impacts of storms on the coastal zone. The data are delivered to the USACE coastal district in which they were collected and to the USGS Center for Coastal and Watershed Studies in St. Petersburg, Florida. The data are archived at the NOAA National Geophysical Data Center and USGS Earth Resources Observation and Science (EROS) Center. All of the data are available online through the NOAA Coastal Services Center Lidar Data Retrieval Tool. The data are also delivered on demand to any local, State, or Federal agency that requests them. In addition to this unique in-house system and capability, the Joint Center maintains surveying contracts to obtain lidar and imagery from industry based systems. In all cases, the Joint Center coordinates operational plans with Federal and State stakeholders, such as USGS, NOAA, FEMA, National Aeronautics and Space Administration (NASA), and others, to prevent duplication and to ensure the widest dissemination of data and resulting products.

3.3.2 USAF and CAP-USAF Auxiliary

The CAP, through a Memorandum of Understanding between the DOD and OFCM, provides light aircraft, aircrews, and communications in support of disaster impact assessment flights. The NWS frequently uses CAP flights to survey ice damming, glacier-dammed lakes, weak levees, remote reservoirs, and tornado tracks. The services that CAP provides are more cost-effective than other available aerial capabilities. The CAP National Operations Center often is able to provide a flight within 24 hours of the request. Any Federal or State agency may request a CAP mission through OFCM by filling out the request form at http://www.ofcm.gov/wg-ndr-psda/index.htm   and submitting it to nws.ofcm.cap@noaa.gov followed by a phone call to (301) 427-2002. The CAP forms are also included in Appendix F.

Photo taken by the Civil Air Patrol during an aerial survey of the Skilak Glacier dammed lake, August, 20, 2010. CAP aerial survey sorties are flown to assess and document water levels of glacier-dammed lakes and assess current hazard levels. Based on this photo, the Skilak lake level was determined to be low and not expected to release later in the year. Image courtesy Civil Air Patrol, Seward Squadron, Alaska Wing.

Funding for CAP must be provided on an annual basis by agencies that use CAP.

The 53 WRS conducts aerial reconnaissance of tropical and extratropical cyclones to provide meteorological data on the geographic position of the storms; central sea-level pressure; vertical profiles of pressure, temperature, dew-point temperature, and wind speed and direction from the surface to flight level; geopotential heights of designated pressure surfaces; and other relevant data.

3.4   DHS/FEMA Capabilities

When the President issues a disaster declaration for an event, FEMA establishes one or more Joint Field Offices (JFOs) to coordinate Federal disaster response and assistance. FEMA also employs a large contingent of temporary Disaster Assistance Employees when necessary, in addition to its authorized permanent staff.

FEMA is organized into eight primary directorates; Logistics Management, Disaster Assistance, Disaster Operations, Grant Programs, National Preparedness, U.S. Fire Administration, National Continuity Programs, and Mitigation. The

The National Response Coordination Center is a multi-agency center than provides overall Federal response coordination. Photo courtesy DHS Office of Operations Coordination.

Mitigation Directorate, which includes the Federal Insurance Administration, coordinates Flood Insurance Studies for the National Flood Insurance Program and Hurricane Evacuation Studies for the National Hurricane Program. The NRCC in Washington, D.C., assists in coordinating efforts among all Federal offices. ESF Coordinator positions within the NRCC are activated for exercises and emergencies. The ESF Coordinators may be of assistance to NPDIA efforts, and Appendix H includes an ESF Coordinator contact sheet. FEMA's website, www.fema.gov, includes the latest FEMA organization chart, as well as articles on FEMA and on Presidentially declared disasters.

Also within the Mitigation Directorate, the Risk Reduction Division, Building Science Branch, in coordination with the JFO Mitigation Branch Director, may elect to deploy a Mitigation Assessment Team (MAT) following a disaster. The objectives of the MAT are to inspect buildings and infrastructure, conduct forensic engineering analyses to determine causes of structural failure and success, and recommend actions that State and local governments, the construction industry, and building code organizations can take to reduce future damages and protect lives and property in hazard areas.

3.5   DOI/USGS Capabilities

Streamflow Monitoring. Data on streamflow (the volume of water passing a specified point on a stream or other channel of moving watrer) are collected primarily by the USGS National Streamflow Information Program through the operation of some 7,500 streamgages and some 27,000 peak-flow-only sites. The streamgaging network is operated by 48 USGS water science centers, whose areas of operation usually correspond to State boundaries, through 160 field offices. Field offices are dispersed throughout the Nation and are strategically located near important rivers and streams. Real-time water-level and flow data for about 6,800 streamgages are available at http://waterdata.usgs.gov/nwis/rt. Interactive maps of the current National and State level flow conditions (relative to flooding or drought) are available at http://water.usgs.gov/waterwatch/. Maps and tables summarizing recent flooding conditions are available at http://water.usgs.gov/cgi-bin/wwdp.

Flood Measurements. Physical measurements of stream depth, width, and water velocities are used to compute flows. Although most flow measurements are made with conventional current meters, a large percentage of high-flow measurements are made by use of Acoustic Doppler Current Meters, which provide rapid and detailed depth, velocity, and flow data. These instruments are routinely deployed to streamgages, but can be used to collect unique data for a variety of situations such as dam— and in some cases levee—breaks or leakages. USGS personnel are often called upon to make emergency measurements of flow by NWS forecasters, USACE dam operators, and emergency management personnel to aid in the management and assessment of floods. Summaries of recent flood measurements (width, depth, velocities, etc.) by State and by streamgage are distributed at http://waterdata.usgs.gov/nwis/measurements.

Flood Forensics. When direct flow measurements are not possible due to short notice or the inaccessibility of the site, the USGS collects detailed high-water mark and steam cross-sectional data and applies hydraulic models to estimate the peak flows. Multiple high-water marks are collected upstream and downstream of constrictions such as bridges or culverts to establish detailed flood profiles for hydraulic models. Accurate determinations of the elevations of the high-water marks are crucial to accurate determination of the flood flows: an elevation difference between high-water marks of just 0.10 feet could result in estimates that are much greater or lower than the actual flows. Hence, high-water marks are surveyed to within +/- 0.01 feet. Indirect flow measurements are computed and summarized in nonpublished reports that may be viewed at the relevant USGS State office. Contact information for these State offices is available at http://water.usgs.gov/district_chief.html.

Storm-Tide Monitoring. The USGS developed a mobile storm-tide network to provide detailed time-series data for selected hurricane landfalls. The network was first deployed to monitor the landfall of Hurricane Rita in Southwest Louisiana in September 2005. It generally consists of about 40 temporary water-level and barometric monitoring instruments. The instruments collect water levels at 30-second intervals before, during, and after surge floods. The instruments can be deployed to observe the interactions of floodwaters with engineered structures and with natural topographic features. Most of the storm-tide sensors log data for later analysis and use, but real-time units have been developed and deployed and could provide real-time on-site reconnaissance for selected facilities. Generally, the instruments can function unattended for 6-8 days. Real-time storm-surge data (for periods during and immediately after the storm) can be viewed by accessing storm-surge sites listed in State streamflow summary tables at webpages with a URL of the form "http://waterdata.usgs.gov/XX/nwis/rt" where "XX" refers to the 2-letter postal abbreviation for the State of interest. As data are corrected and finalized, they are published in online data series reports with ASCII character, tab-delimited or fixed-column formats at http://water.usgs.gov/osw/programs/storm_surge.html.

Rapid-Deployable Gages. Often data are needed at ungaged sites. To provide data at short notice, the USGS developed small, rapidly deployable streamgages that provide real-time water-level data. These devices are equipped with satellite transmitters for real-time transmissions and solar panels and batteries to extend the deployment indefinitely. Data from these gages are available at webpages with a URL of the form: "http://waterdata.usgs.gov/XX/nwis/rt" where "XX" refers to the 2-letter postal abbreviation for the State of interest.

The USGS has developed new rapidly deployable, mobile streamgages to provide short-term water-level data to critical areas lacking permanent streamgages. Image provided by USGS Office of Surface Water.

Flood Documentation. Personnel at the USGS Water Science Center are trained to flag and document high-water marks. USGS techniques differ from those more commonly used to develop flood-inundation maps. More effort is expended to flag multiple high-water marks needed to profile flood levels upstream and downstream of stream constrictions and the elevations are surveyed to within 0.01 feet to permit calibration of flood models. However, the USGS has assisted some flood documentation efforts in which the USGS effort was limited to flagging so that others could level in elevations using more rapid, but less accurate, Global Positioning System (GPS) techniques. When the data are used by the USGS to construct flood maps, the data are available through USGS publications at http://pubs.er.usgs.gov/usgspubs/recentpubs.jsp.

Shoreline Change. Through the Coastal and Marine Geology Program, the USGS Geologic Division investigates the geologic impacts of extreme storms and hurricanes on the physical coastal environment. A major objective of these investigations is to improve the capability to predict coastal erosion and other coastal changes caused by extreme storms. To conduct these investigations, Geologic Division personnel employ aerial photography and oceanographic techniques, emerging technologies like airborne scanning laser (e.g., LIDAR), recently available declassified instruments and data, and a USGS network of tide and environmental sensors. State-of-the-art research vessels, GPS satellites, and side-scan survey and velocity measurement equipment are used to collect post-storm data. Images and data are available at http://coastal.er.usgs.gov/shoreline-change/.

3.6   DOT/FHWA Capabilities

The FHWA, though not a current participant in the NPDIA, is expected to become more involved in the future. While FHWA has no statutory requirements to acquire environmental data following significant storm events, it does work with State and local departments of transportation, which are building such capabilities for their areas of responsibility. These sites, which monitor parts of the highway system, could eventually be used in the storm event data acquisition process.

3.7   Capabilities of Affiliated Organizations

3.7.1 AAWE Capabilities

AAWE was originally established in 1966 as the Wind Engineering Research Council to promote and disseminate technical information in the research community. In 1983 the name was changed to American Association for Wind Engineering, and AAWE was incorporated as a nonprofit professional organization. The multidisciplinary field of wind engineering considers problems related to wind and associated water loads on buildings and structures, societal impact of winds, hurricane and tornado risk assessment, cost-benefit analysis, codes and standards, dispersion of urban and industrial pollution, wind energy, and urban aerodynamics.

Several of the AAWE partner institutions have a coordinated program to place robust and portable

Data observed using the Texas Tech StickNet system for wind, rain, relative humidity, and barometric pressure can be used in damage assessments. Photo courtesy Sarah Dillingham, Texas Tech University weather monitors in the path of hurricanes at land fall. Louisiana State University and Texas Technological University have also been using before- and after-storm satellite imagery to assess storm damage and to develop algorithms and procedures to gather high volume and high quality performance assessment data that complement on-ground data collection efforts.

3.7.2 COPRI Capabilities

COPRI capabilities were under development at the time that this version of the NPDIA was undergoing final review.

3.7.3 DHC Capabilities

The CSWR, Oklahoma University, and the University of Alabama at Huntsville—all members of the DHC—have mobile radar capabilities that add to the data collection strength of mobile anemometer towers. The mobile radar equipment has the ability to give the hurricane windfield three-dimensional depth, which anemometers cannot do. These radars will assist in gathering offshore wind speed information, which is now only possible for locations just offshore. Radar data on the vertical windfield could give us a much better idea of the wind layers above the ground layer where the built environment is located.

The University of Florida (UF) manages the Florida Coastal Monitoring Program, a research program with the goal of characterizing the intensity and behavior of land-falling hurricanes with direct measurement of wind speed, wind direction, pressure, humidity and temperature at multiple ground level locations(10 meter) in the path of land fall via five portable weather monitoring platforms. Texas Tech University, Louisiana State University, and Clemson University also participate in this project with additional portable monitoring assets. Much of the data are relayed in real time to a public access web site and via direct push to researchers in

Retrieving a shallow water wave monitor.
Photo courtesy University of Notre Dame.

NOAA's Hurricane Research Division. Since 1999, the high reliability of research-grade instrumentation and hurricane-hardened portable platforms has yielded the most dependable source of direct-measured overland ground-level wind data. Additional near-shore wave and surge monitoring assets have been developed by the University of Notre Dame to provide water elevation datasets that complement both the wind data collection as well as USGS surge monitoring efforts. UF and the University of Notre Dame retain faculty that lead the current state of the art in coastal process modeling, including hurricane surge and inland flooding from heavy rainfall. UF and Florida Institute of Technology also deploy pressure measurement packages on the roofs and walls of homes along the coast of Florida to directly monitor the wind pressure experienced by structural components during land-falling hurricanes. This work is a leading source of information for refining the next generation of wind load provisions for minimum building code standards.

UF also offers an extensive infrastructure of laboratory apparatus to evaluate structural performance characteristics in hurricane winds and wind driven rain. The full-scale hurricane simulator at UF provides a means to develop and evaluate new construction methods as well as retrofit mitigation measures on existing building inventory. Home builders and product manufacturers work with the UF faculty to identify outstanding performance issues and identify cost effective and practical solutions to weaknesses in building performance.

During the process of equipment retrieval in the immediate aftermath of a land-falling hurricane, university teams provide an assessment of infrastructure damage prior to data-altering activities such as clean-up, blue-tarp, etc. In some circumstances (e.g., after Hurricane Charlie in 2004), UF and other university research groups remained in the field after equipment retrieval to conduct a more thorough quantitative building performance study.

3.8   Requirements

Table 3-1 outlines the disaster impact assessment requirements of each of the Federal agencies and affiliated organizations participating in the WG/DIAP.

Table 3-1 Disaster Impact Assessment Requirements

Fed. dept. or affiliated organization	Subentity	Disaster impact assessment requirements
USDA	NRCS	NRCS is typically required to make post-storm analyses to determine extent of damage to installed conservation measures so that they can be restored to pre-storm conditions.
DOC	NOAA/ NWS	NWS requires all available records that define the impact, extent, timing, and intensity of significant natural hazard episodes such as floods, tropical cyclones, extratropical cyclones, tornadoes and other severe convective events, katabatic winds, and tsunamis.
	NOAA/ NOS	to be determined
	NOAA/ CSC	CSC requires forecast data from NWS to develop before, during, and after forecast maps for the NOAA ICC and DHS/FEMA. In the past, this has been done on an as-needed basis, driven by mission assignment from FEMA before a land-falling storm.
	NOAA/ CO-OPS	CO-OPS requires all available NOAA-collected oceanographic and meteorological data (historical and real-time), predictions, nowcasts, forecasts, and high- water mark elevations.
	NOAA/ OR&R	to be determined
	NOAA/ NGS	NGS requires the geographic extent of the requested imagery, and those data necessary to conduct aerial survey operations, current aviation weather reports, and aviation weather forecasts to facilitate accurate data collection following an emergency.
DOC	NIST	In wind-related disasters, NIST needs all available records of wind speeds (from both ground stations and aircraft), barometric pressure measurements, and radar images from which to reconstruct the surface wind field are essential.
		Aerial photographs of sufficient resolution to show damage and debris distribution and extent of storm-surge effects are of considerable value. In the case of damage to major structures, detailed site studies, followed by structural analyses, are performed.
DOD	USAF/ CAP and 53 WRS	CAP and 53 WRS have no individual requirements for data.

Table 3-1 Disaster Impact Assessment Requirements

Fed. dept. or affiliated organization	Subentity	Disaster impact assessment requirements
DOD	U.S. Army/ USACE	USACE requires environmental data to support the following missions: • Coastal—shore protection, beach preservation and restoration, coastal navigation, environmental and water quality monitoring • Estuarine— navigation, environmental and water quality monitoring • Riverine— inland navigation, flooding and stream bank erosion control, environmental and water quality monitoring • Reservoir control— reservoir level monitoring, catchment rate determination Any data that contribute to performance of these missions are of value. Types of data include: tropical and extratropical storm-surge water levels and waves; storm-generated coastal current and morphological changes from imagery and from topographic/ bathymetric surveys: estuarine tidal inundation: precipitation-generated estuarine inflow: riverine flooding events: and reservoir overtopping.
DHS	FEMA	Perishable storm data are needed to support FEMA's mission. Data include high-water marks in riverine and coastal-flooded areas; perishable wind-waterline and/or inland wind impact data. Reconnaissance data are required during or within 12-24 hours after a storm event; such data are obtained by radar, reconnaissance flights, satellites, and water-level gauges that transmit their data. Wind-waterline data— the line that distinguishes damages caused by water damage versus wind damage— has immediate application for insurance claims. FEMA also requires analyzed fields of maximum surface wind speeds caused by tornadoes, tropical storms, hurricanes, and winter storms. The information in these fields is typically derived from surface observations and available Doppler radar data. Water-level, wind-speed, and wind-waterline data have been used to prepare the Hazard Analysis section in Post-Storm Assessment reports following major hurricanes. Water-level and wind-speed data from recent tropical storms and hurricanes have been used by the Storm-Surge Group at the Tropical Prediction Center/National Hurricane Center to verify hurricane and winter-storm computer simulation and prediction models. These studies are sponsored by FEMA and are primarily used to verify the predicted maximum storm-surge heights derived from the NWS's Sea, Lake, and Overland Surges from Hurricanes (SLOSH) model. SLOSH is used to make predictions of maximum storm-surge heights for classes of hurricanes striking a given coastal area. Information derived from SLOSH is used to identify vulnerable populations that must be evacuated and critical facilities that need to be protected from storm-surge flooding in coastal communities. These data will continue to be needed in future disasters to verify SLOSH model output and to support other FEMA mission requirements. Perishable, riverine, and coastal-flooding data are used by the National Flood Insurance Program to calibrate and verify hydrologic and hydraulic models used in Flood Insurance Studies to establish the one-percent chance base-flood elevations shown on Flood Insurance Rate Maps. Flooding information caused by tsunami events affecting the U.S. West Coast and Pacific islands is also needed to prepare tsunami hazard maps. Existing water-level data documenting such events are insufficient and are critically needed to verify computer models used for tsunami run-up predictions.
DOI	USGS	The operational needs of the USGS during pre- and post-storm activities include access to forecasts, flood reports, and warning statements issued by NWS; road condition and

Table 3-1 Disaster Impact Assessment Requirements

Fed. dept. or affiliated organization	Subentity	Disaster impact assessment requirements
		access reports issued by transportation officials, emergency management operation centers, and law enforcement agencies; and identification/authorization credentials needed to quickly access flooded area. Potential data needs from other agencies include aerial photography, field support with small aircraft (fixed wing and helicopter), and analytical model results of storm surge and waves. Photographs of streamgaging stations and bridge sites would be useful during and immediately after floods, when a survey and computation of discharge could be made after the flood.
		Riverine Flooding—The USGS requires assistance in the form of flood forecasts that include specific locations and timing. Photographs, bridge cross-section surveys, and information about timing, etc. obtained from local residents are often helpful forensic determinations.
		Land-falling Tropical Storms—The USGS requires assistance in the form of hurricane and surge forecasts that include specific locations and timing. Photographs, bridge cross-section surveys, and information about timing, etc. obtained from local residents are often helpful. The USGS will partner with other agencies in deploying devices and obtaining survey data and high-water marks.
DOT	FHWA	To be determined. (Although not a current participant, FHWA is expected to become more involved in the future)
AAWE		Given the breadth of potential services provided by AAWE members for extreme event investigations, specific data needs cannot be delineated. Typically the most pressing requirement will be logistics coordination, support for the data collection, and a supervisory authority to determine the specific data collection mission.
COPRI		To be determined.
DHC		The consortium has no specific data requirements, but it does recognize the need to establish a consistent framework for reporting collected field data. Coordination with NOAA Hurricane Research Division and NWS officials is essential for proper placement of portable monitoring assets.

EVENT SUMMARIES

4.1 General

For a storm event that involves more than one agency, OFCM will compile an event summary when the majority of data collection is complete and submitted. OFCM will consolidate all participant event information related to the event. Individual agencies should complete event summaries as directed by internal guidance and then forward them to OFCM to be compiled into the overall event summary. The summaries will include a concise description of the event, interpretive information, and supporting data, as well as pointers to where the actual event data resides. Examples of event summaries prepared by individual agencies that include actual data include the NWS Service Assessment of the La Plata, Maryland, Tornado Outbreak of April 28, 2002; FEMA MAT and Building Performance Assessment Team reports; data gathered by the USACE; and reports of water levels associated with hurricanes and tropical storms from NOS/CO-OPS.

The interpretive information and supporting data in an event summary will be directed at satisfying the requirements and needs of secondary users. These users include those whose requirements are met by processed data and/or composite images. Users requiring access to unprocessed data (i.e., disk data files) will be directed to the acquiring agency. Many or most of the single agency summaries can be found by accessing the agency's URL listed in Appendix C. The final consolidated event summaries can be found at: http://www.ofcm.noaa.gov/wg-diap/eventsum.htm.

4.2 Content Outline

The WG/DIAP recommends that the following sections be included in an event summary report:
  a. Executive summary
  b. Event description and its impact
  c. Event analysis
  d. Description of agency responses
  e. Description of data acquired, availability, and deposition status
  f. Supporting documentation (e.g., eyewitness accounts)
  g. Conclusions, findings, and/or recommendations, if appropriate

4.3 Examples of Past Disaster Impact Assessments

Appendix K includes examples of past disaster impact assessments for Hurricanes Hugo, Andrew, and Katrina and for Midwest Flooding.

APPENDICES

APPENDIX A
NPDIA SUPPORT FOR EMERGENCY SUPPORT FUNCTIONS

With the addition of real-time data, this plan supports nearly all Emergency Support Functions (ESFs) in the National Response Framework in either a real-time or long-term application. Descriptions of the support provided to the ESFs by this plan are listed in the table below.

ESF	Real-time Support to ESFs	Long-term Support to ESFs
ESF #1 – Transportation	Pre-storm deployments could yield on-site wind and flooding data needed to refine road and bridge conditions and aide routing of evacuations and relief supplies before, during, and after, the events.	Wind speed, direction, and damage data and high-water elevation and flooding data needed to define event strength and frequency and assess infra-structure performance and safe window of operation (e.g. bridge crossings). Such information could lead to more robust transportation systems and better models of system performance during severe weather.
ESF #2 – Communications	Continuous data during a storm event can be used to anticipate and respond to impacts to communication systems.	Weather and water impact information can be used to prevent placement of communications equip-ment in flood areas and can be used to understand the environmental impacts on communications equipment.
ESF #3 – Public Works and Engineering	Real-time instrumentation could provide data that would improve estimates of infrastructure damage, due to winds, waves and high water/surge.	Improve characterization of wind speed, durations and damage and flood extent, depth, and volume and led to improve infrastructure and damage estimation models. The data also provides the means for development of more accurate and risk consistent building codes and standards than currently exist
ESF #4 – Firefighting	Not Applicable	Not Applicable
ESF #5 – Emergency Management	Pre-storm deployments could yield on-site wind, waves and flooding/surge/water-level data needed to estimate the spatial extent and severity of storm impacts throughout the event and better allocate resources.	Weather and water data could yield better models for predicting damages from storms.
ESF #6 – Mass Care, Emergency Assistance, Housing, and Human Services	Weather and water data could be used for planning the location of and timing for set up of ESF #6 facilities.	Weather and water data could provide Preparedness and Mitigation Planning to reduce or prevent future damage by similar events
ESF #7 – Logistics Management and Resource Support	The real-time information collected and disseminated directly supports comprehensive, national incident logistics planning, management, and sustainment capability	
ESF #8 – Public Health and Medical Services	Not Applicable	Not Applicable

ESF	Real-time Support to ESFs	Long-term Support to ESFs
ESF #9 – Search and Rescue	The real-time information collected and disseminated directly supports life-saving assistance, search and rescue operations by providing situational awareness of current conditions.	
ESF #10 – Oil and Hazardous Materials Response	Water-level and wind speed and direction data (e.g. surface currents) collected and disseminated directly supports oil and hazardous materials (chemical, biological, radiological, etc.) response and environmental short- and long-term cleanup.	Hydrodynamic models and historical wind and water data can support preparedness and mitigation planning for potential future events.
ESF #11 – Agriculture and Natural Resources	Not applicable	The collected and disseminated information directly supports natural and cultural resources and historic properties protection and restoration.
ESF #12 – Energy	Not applicable	Wind speed, direction, and damage data and high-water elevation and flooding data needed to characterize event strength and frequency and infrastructure performance. Such information could lead to more robust energy systems and better models of system performance during severe weather.
ESF #13 – Public Safety and Security	Weather and water impact information collected and disseminated directly supports public safety and security support as well as support to access, evacuation, traffic, and crowd control.	Development of hazard resilient infrastructure via direct measurement of severe hazard loads directly supports public safety and security during and after events
ESF #14 – Long-Term Community Recovery	Not applicable	Weather and water impact information collected and disseminated directly supports social and economic community impact assessments, long-term community recovery assistance to States, local governments, and the private sector as well as analysis and review of mitigation program implementation.
ESF #15 – External Affairs	Weather and water impact information collected and disseminated directly supports emergency public information and protective action guidance, media and community relations, Congressional and international affairs as well as tribal and insular affairs.	Weather and water impact information collected and disseminated directly supports emergency public information and protective action guidance, media and community relations, Congressional and international affairs as well as tribal and insular affairs.

APPENDIX B
AGENCY/ENTITY AUTHORITY AND MISSION STATEMENTS

Department of Agriculture (USDA)

Natural Resources Conservation Service (NRCS)

The USDA Natural Resources Conservation Service (NRCS) leads the federal commitment to the conservation of all natural resources by ensuring private lands are conserved, restored, and more resilient to environmental challenges, like climate change. NRCS works with landowners through conservation planning and assistance designed to benefit the soil, water, air, plants, and animals that result in productive lands and healthy ecosystems. The NRCS provides technical and financial assistance through local conservation districts to land users, communities, watershed groups, federal and state agencies, American Indian tribes, and others at their request. At the local level, the NRCS staff works alongside state and local conservation staff and volunteers in a partnership to care for natural resources on private lands. The NRCS develops comprehensive technical guidance for conservation planning and assistance.

Contained in the Rural Development Act of 1972, Public Law 92-419, Sec. 302, Title III (7 USC 1010a), August 30, 1972, which authorizes a land inventory and monitoring program, including studies and surveys of erosion, sediment damage, flood plain identification, and land use changes and trends.

The Watershed Protection and Flood Prevention Act (PL 83-566, Statute 606) authorizes the Secretary of Agriculture to cooperate with state and local governments in planning and conducting improvements for soil conservation and other purposes.

The Snow Survey and Water Supply Forecasting Program, administered by NRCS, is found in the Code of Federal Regulations 7 CFS 612. NRCS is charged with the responsibility of collection snow data to develop monthly water supply forecasts from January through June in partnership with the National Weather Service, and to maintain and make publically available the database.

Department of Commerce (DOC)

National Oceanic and Atmospheric Administration

To understand and predict changes in Earth's environment and conserve and manage coastal and marine resources to meet our Nation's economic, social, and environmental needs.

National Weather Service

The National Weather Service (NWS) provides weather, hydrologic, and climate forecasts and warnings for the United States, its territories, adjacent waters and ocean areas, for the protection of life and property and the enhancement of the national economy. NWS data and products form a national information database and infrastructure which can be used by other governmental agencies, the private sector, the public, and the global community.

National Ocean Service (NOS)

The NOS works to provide science-based solutions through collaborative partnerships to address evolving economic, environmental, and social pressures on our oceans and coasts. This includes protecting coastal communities, monitoring our oceans and coasts, promoting safe, efficient and environmentally sound marine transportation, reducing ocean and coastal health risks, and protecting coastal and marine places.

NOS/Coastal Services Center (CSC)

The CSC supports the environmental, social, and economic well being of the coast by linking people, information, and technology. The CSC helps communities prepare for and respond to coastal hazards. The Center's coastal hazards toolkit of services for state and local organizations allows users to quickly find the hazard-related information they need, effectively apply it, and visually showcase the results to their constituents and other end users. The coastal hazards toolkit of services provides data and information, data analysis, and visualization tools. These products and services help coastal regions prepare for and react to both chronic episodic events and longer-term climate change issues such as sea-level rise.

NOS/Center for Operational Oceanographic Products and Services

The Center for Operational Oceanographic Products and Services (CO-OPS) provides the national infrastructure, science, and technical expertise to monitor, assess, and distribute tide, current, water level, and other coastal oceanographic products and services that support NOAA's mission of environmental stewardship and environmental assessment and prediction. CO-OPS provides operationally sound observations and monitoring capabilities coupled with operational Nowcast Forecast modeling. Mission: To serve as the authoritative source for accurate, reliable, and timely tide, water level, current, and other oceanographic information to support safe and efficient navigation, sound ecosystem stewardship, coastal hazard preparedness and response, and the understanding of climate change.

NOS/Office of Response and Restoration

The Office of Response and Restoration (OR&R) protects coastal and marine resources, mitigates threats, reduces harm, and restores ecological function. The Office provides comprehensive solutions to environmental hazards caused by oil, chemicals, and marine debris.

NOS/National Geodetic Survey

Authority: ***COAST AND GEODETIC SURVEY ACT - 33 U.S.C. 883 et seq,***
HYDROGRAPHIC SERVICE IMPROVEMENT ACT OF 1998 and 2002 Amendments - 33 U.S.C.
883a et seq
National Response Framework – ESF's # 1, 11, 13

Mission Statement: The mission of the National Geodetic Survey (NGS) is understood to be: 1) To define, maintain and provide access to the National Spatial Reference System (including the National Shoreline) to meet our nation's economic, social, and environmental needs, and 2) To be a world leader in geospatial activities, including the development and promotion of standards, specifications, and guidelines.

National Institute of Standards and Technology

Contained in the National Bureau of Standards Authorizing Act of 1986: "The National Bureau of Standards, on its own initiative, ... may initiate and conduct investigations to determine the causes of structural failures in structures which are used or occupied by the general public."

Department of Defense (DOD)

U.S. Army Corps of Engineers (USACE)

U.S. Air Force (USAF), Civil Air Patrol (CAP)-USAF Auxiliary

The DOD is represented by elements of the U.S. Army and U.S. Air Force, primarily by the USACE and the Civil Air Patrol (CAP), a civilian auxiliary of the U.S. Air Force. The CAP and the Air Force Reserve Command's 53rd Weather Reconnaissance Squadron (53 WRS) serve principally in a supporting role to the other participating agencies. The USACE has primary responsibility for construction and maintenance of marine navigation in public waterways and coastal storm protection projects on public lands. The USACE post-event activities are coordinated through the Office of Chief of Engineers, and the Engineer Research and Development Center (ERDC).

US Army Corps of Engineers
Public Law 71 (Coastal and Tidal Areas - Survey - Damages), 84th Congress, 1955.

US Air Force
Memorandum of Agreement between the USAF Reserve and NOAA dated May 4, 1992.

Civil Air Patrol
The Civil Air Patrol (CAP) is chartered under 36 U.S.C. 201 et. seq. and is a civilian auxiliary of the USAF. The USAF is authorized under 10 U.S.C. 9441 to use the services of the CAP to fulfill its non-combat missions. The 5-year umbrella Memorandum of Understanding between the DoD and OFCM was signed 4 May 2007.

Department of Homeland Security (DHS)

Federal Emergency Management Agency (FEMA)

DHS and its ancillary FEMA are the federal coordinating agencies that respond to major disasters or threats in the United States and its territories. FEMA provides response and recovery and hazard mitigation assistance, emergency management preparedness training, flood insurance, and funding for related studies and services. Headquartered in Washington, DC, FEMA has 10 regional offices, with field offices and special facilities located nationwide.

Contained in the agency charter as "... providing the leadership and support to reduce the loss of life and property and protect our institutions from all types of hazards through a comprehensive, risk-based, all hazards emergency program of mitigation, preparedness, response, and recovery."

Department of the Interior (DOI)

U.S. Geological Survey (USGS)

USGS is the principal Earth science agency responsible for collection, assessment, and dissemination of information, regarding the geology, topography, mineral resources, hydrology, and biology of the U.S. The USGS is a nationally recognized provider of water data and information for use by others to design, operate, manage, and regulate water resources, establish floodplain boundaries, issue flood warnings and river forecasts, and manage emergency operations. USGS real-time and long-term flow records and stage-discharge relationships (ratings) are key inputs for NWS forecast models and peak-flow data are fundamental to flood-frequency analyses on which depend the design of dams and the delineation of flood-insurance rate maps.

The Water Resources Division of the USGS is responsible for the coordination of the water-data acquisition activities of all federal agencies as mandated by Office of Management and Budget Memorandum No. M-92.01.

Department of Transportation (DOT)

The Federal Highway Administration (FHWA)

The FHWA, though not a current participant, is expected to become more involved in the future. While they have no requirements to acquire environmental data following significant storm events, they work with state and local DOTs who are building the capabilities to do so. These sites, which monitor the highway system, could eventually be used in the storm event data acquisition process.

Affiliated Organizations

The American Association for Wind Engineering

The American Association for Wind Engineering (AAWE) was originally established as the Wind Engineering Research Council in 1966 to promote and disseminate technical information in the research community. In 1983 the name was changed to American Association for Wind Engineering and incorporated as a nonprofit professional organization. The multi-disciplinary field of wind engineering considers problems related to wind and associated water loads and penetrations for buildings and structures, societal impact of winds, hurricane and tornado risk assessment, cost-benefit analysis, codes and standards, dispersion of urban and industrial pollution, wind energy and urban aerodynamics. AAWE membership consists of academic and industry experts in wind effects on structures, and stands ready to assist in the event of wind disasters.

Coasts, Oceans, Ports and Rivers Institute (COPRI)

COPRE is one of the American Society of Civil Engineering (ASCE)'s eight institutes. COPRI focuses on specific civil engineering specialties by centering on the technical, educational, scientific and professional issues unique to coastal, ocean, ports, waterways, wetlands and riverine environments. COPRI strives to advance and disseminate scientific and engineering knowledge to its diverse membership.

Digital Hurricane Consortium (DHC)

Faculty from participating universities including University of Florida (UF), Texas Tech University (TTU), Louisiana State University (LSU), University of Notre Dame (ND), the University of Alabama at Huntsville (UAH), Oklahoma University (OU), the Center for Severe Weather Research (CSWR), Colorado University (CU), Clemson University, Florida International University (FIU), and the Applied Technology Council (ATC) have come together to form the Digital Hurricane Consortium. The participating members have formed an alliance that is intended to better respond to severe weather events, especially hurricanes by mobilizing field deployed equipment to collect wind field and storm surge measurements that are extremely useful in determining not only the strength of the event but how the built environment responded to the event in terms of damage. Expertise in the consortium includes wind and structural engineering, coastal process monitoring and modeling (flooding and surge), atmospheric science, field measurement of hurricane winds, and structural vulnerability and mitigation assessments.

APPENDIX C
LINKS FOR PARTICIPATING
FEDERAL AGENCIES AND ENTITIES

American Association for Wind Engineering	www.aawe.org
Center for Operational Oceanic Products and Services	www.tidesandcurrents.noaa.gov
Coastal Services Center	www.csc.noaa.gov
Coasts, Oceans, Ports and Rivers Institute	http://content.coprinstitute.org/
Civil Air Patrol Request Form	http://www.ofcm.noaa.gov/wg-diap/reference.htm
Consolidated WG/DIAP Metadata	http://www.ofcm.noaa.gov/wg-diap/metadata.htm
Department of Homeland Security	http://www.dhs.gov/index.shtm
Digital Hurricane Consortium	http://www.digitalhurricane.org
Event Summaries	http://www.ofcm.noaa.gov/wg-diap/eventsum.htm
Federal Highway Administration	www.fhwa.dot.gov
Federal Emergency Management Agency	www.fema.gov
FEMA Building Performance Assessment Team	www.fema.gov/mit/bpat/bp_faqs.htm
Homeland Security Information Network	https://government.hsin.gov
National Institute of Standards and Technology	www.nist.gov
National Oceanic and Atmospheric Administration	www.noaa.gov
National Weather Service	www.nws.noaa.gov
National Geodetic Survey	www.ngs.noaa.gov
National Ocean Service	www.nos.noaa.gov
National Resources Conservation Service	www.nrcs.usda.gov

Office of the Federal Coordinator for Meteorological
    Services and Supporting Research   www.ofcm.gov

University Wind Research Consortium   http://fcmp.ce.ufl.edu/
                                        http://www.atmo.ttu.edu

US Air Force   www.af.mil
                               www.hurricanehunters.com

US Army Corps of Engineers   www.usace.army.mil

US Department of Agriculture   www.usda.gov

US Department of Transportation   www.dot.gov

US Geological Survey   www.usgs.gov

APPENDIX D
NATIONAL OCEANIC AND ATMOSPHERIC ADMINISTRATION
INTERNAL PROCEDURES

National Weather Service policy for tsunami surveys is available at:
http://www.nws.noaa.gov/directives/sym/pd01007003curr.pdf

National Weather Service policy for Service Assessments is available at:
http://www.nws.noaa.gov/directives/sym/pd01016006curr.pdf

National Weather Service policy for Post Storm Data Acquisition is available at:
http://www.nws.noaa.gov/directives/sym/pd01016004curr.pdf

National Ocean Service Support for Post-Storm Data Acquisition and Mapping

1.) Via the NOAA Emergency Response Program (EMR) the NOAA Coastal Services Center provides training modules on how to access, process, and use NOAA forecast and observation data in geospatial formats before, during, and after a storm event. Primary audience for training module is DHS/FEMA personnel, NOAA ICC staff, and NOAA HSOC staff for creation of situational awareness maps for decision briefings. http://www.csc.noaa.gov/storm_info/tutorial.html

2.) The NOAA Tides Online Web page provides users with immediate graphical and tabular water-level and meteorological data from NOS water-level stations located along the projected path of severe storms such as hurricanes. Products include time series graphs of observed vs. predicted astronomical tides and various other meteorological variables, including wind speed and direction. This information is updated hourly during calm conditions, and every eighteen minutes in storm surge mode. The CO-OPS Continuous Operational Real-Time Monitoring System (CORMS) program monitors the operational status and data quality of all stations in both the national Physical Oceanographic Real-Time System (PORTS) and the National Water Level Observation Network (NWLON). CORMS is manned 24 hours a day by contract watchstanders on 12-hour shifts. Once the NHC/TPC identifies a tropical storm, CORMS watchstanders begin tracking the storm and reporting its progress to CO-OPS personnel. As soon as the storm approaches the coast, the watchstanders manually call the data collection platforms (DCPs) at stations within the projected track, and trigger the DCPs to transmit data every 18 minutes rather than the typical one- or three-hour intervals. Once triggered, a station becomes listed as currently active on the page. Stations may also become listed if water levels exceed predetermined upper and lower limits coded into the software (site specific). This "storm surge mode" is an automatic process. CO-OPS also provides a series (four times per day) of storm surge "Quicklook" Web-based products during each event that shows summaries of significant storm surges and meteorological data observed at NOAA-operated and NOAA-partnership stations within the areas affected. http://tidesonline.nos.noaa.gov/

3.) The NOAA National Geodetic Survey provides aerial remote sensing support for hurricane recovery and rebuilding efforts including data acquisition, processing, and dissemination.

4.) Under the NOAA Emergency Response Program (EMR) NOS provides technical assistance for disaster response, recovery and rebuilding efforts to include coastal resource management, support to application of Geographic Information System and remote sensing data, planning process support, (includes community participation process design and facilitation,) assist with recovery project development.

5.) Under the NOAA Emergency Response Program (EMR) NOS provides real-time water levels, currents, winds and other oceanographic and meteorological measurements for major US port areas." Center for Operational Oceanographic Products and Services (CO-OPS). This infrastructure acquires and disseminates observations and predictions of data and information necessary to ensure secure, safe, efficient environmentally sound maritime commerce. The real-time tides and current critical infrastructure supports national security, safe navigation, sustainable coastal communities, and disaster response. Real-time water levels and current information are essential to post-incident environmental impacts and waterway evacuation.

6.) Under the NOAA Emergency Response Program (EMR) NOS coordinates and/or conduct side scan and multi-beam surveys in impacted regions to identify marine debris fields and other obstructions in-navigable areas, including navigation channels, approaches to impacted ports, and critical fishing habitat areas.

7.) Under the NOAA Emergency Response Program (EMR) NOS responds to and mitigate the consequences of spills and other hazards that threaten coastal environments." ...providing accurate, timely and relevant scientific advice to organizations charged with responding to and mitigating the consequences of spills and other hazards that threaten coastal environments and communities. The HAZMAT scientific team provides key technical advice during spills of oil or hazardous materials in the coastal zone. To do this, the HAZMAT team is on-call 24-hours a day, every day of the year. HAZMAT also responds to other technological and natural coastal hazards such as hurricanes and airplane crashes. HAZMAT carries out these functions under the National Response Plan and the National Oil and Hazardous Substances Pollution Contingency Plan. This group operates CAMEO, a well known NOAA software program which is in use at over 10,000 places. CAMEO (Computer Aided Management to Emergency Operations) provides first responders and emergency planners with information to quickly respond to chemical accidents.

APPENDIX E
UNITED STATES GEOLOGICAL SURVEY
INTERNAL PROCEDURES

Generic Flood Plan for Documenting Storm-Surge High-Water Marks

I. PROJECT ORGANIZATION

   A. Project Oversight and Coordination

      1. Water Science Center (WSC) Flood Coordinator

         a. Monitor network - Determine status of satellite link and data collection platforms. Determine status of other gauging stations in affected area.

         b. Flood measurement - Determine if flooding has occurred and oversee the organization of field crews and technicians to make flood measurements on streams impacted by heavy precipitation if needed.

         c. Storm surge - Organize personnel for the collection of high-water marks in the impacted area. Assign someone the duty of project chief and authorize to direct other personnel as needed.

         e. Survey contacts - Determine the need for additional personnel and make appropriate contacts to temporarily obtain personnel from other WSCs.

         f. Other contacts - Notify appropriate agencies as per the decisions of the OFCM Post-Storm Data Acquisitions Working Group.

II. STORM-SURGE DOCUMENTATION

   A. Advance Planning

      1. Maps - Several sets of quad maps of coastal areas could be obtained and kept on hand in case of a hurricane event.

      2. Transects - Coastal transects can be defined prior to a hurricane event.

      3. Bench marks - Information for benchmarks located in coastal counties can be obtained prior to the hurricane event. Sources include the National Geodetic Survey and county engineers.

      4. Other agencies - Information about other agencies that would be involved in a hurricane event could be compiled prior to a hurricane event. This would include local agencies such as levee districts and county engineers.

   B. Equipment

1. Transportation and lodging - At least one vehicle is needed for each field crew. Personnel on loan from neighboring WSCs should be encouraged to bring a vehicle if needed. Boats may be needed to reach remote areas. Lodging in the impacted are may be difficult to obtain due to the influx of insurance adjusters, utility repairmen, etc. Reservations for a lodging as close as possible to the impacted area should be made immediately after the storm.

2. Maps, transacts, and benchmarks - Each field crew should be given a set of quad maps for their assigned area. If available, maps and information about benchmarks in their area should also be given to each crew.

3. Surveying equipment - Each field crew should have at least one field notebook, level, tripod, rod, 50-ft. steel tape, and folding engineers rule for surveying. They should also have an adequate supply of spray paint, chalk, magic markers, flagging, stakes, nails, cold chisel, and a hammer for flagging and surveying the high-water marks. A carpenters level is also handy for carrying marks around comers.

4. Cameras - Each field crew should have a camera. The disposable cameras work well, but each photograph should be documented in the field book. Polaroid cameras, that give you the photo on the spot, also work well because you can put information directly on the photo. However, getting reprints of these can be costly.

5. Mobile phones - Mobile phones can be useful to field crews. The field crews need to make daily contact with the project chief, at least in the initial stages of the investigation, and the impacted areas have often lost phone services.

6. Global Positioning Systems - The portable "Pathfinder" units work extremely well for documenting high-water mark locations. Elevation measurements made using the larger GPS systems may not produce the level of accuracy required for the study.

7. Other - Field crews may need rubber boots, rain gear, insect repellent, shovels, and machetes. In addition, field crews may need documents or permits from appropriate agencies authorizing passage through roadblocks into stricken areas.

C. High-water Mark Data Collection

1. Project Chief

   a. Assignment of duties - The project chief is responsible for the assignment of areas or transacts to the field crews and the designation of a leader for each crew. The project chief is also responsible for providing the field crews with benchmark information and necessary maps.

   b. Data checks - The project chief is responsible for collecting and checking field data from the crews as it becomes available. Make copies of field notes as they become available. Transfer data from field maps to a master set and check for completeness of coverage and cohesiveness of adjacent high-water mark elevations. The project chief is also responsible for collecting all field notebooks, maps, and film at the end of the surveying phase of the project.

c. Field perspective - The project chief should spend most of his time in the field collecting data so that he becomes completely familiar with the situation, and can be in constant contact with the other field crews.

d. Local agencies - The project chief should meet with local, State, and federal agencies with common interests in storm-surge documentation and compare notes and ideas.

2. Field crews

   a. Equipment - Field crews should be responsible for obtaining and maintaining the necessary vehicles and equipment.

   b. Lodging - Field crews should make the necessary lodging arrangements as soon as possible after they receive their assignments.

   c. Documentation - Each crew is responsible for the full and complete documentation of the storm-surge in their assigned area.

3. Flagging high-water marks

   a. Locating marks - Talking to locals in the area is the best way to find out about the storm-surge in an area. Stop and ask when you see someone outside of his or her house or business. Once you've identified one high-water mark, it is not too difficult to track the highwater along the remainder of the transect.

   b. Transits –Try to establish a transit lines so that transits are grouped closely (every mile or so) near the area of center of the landfall and every 5-10 miles along remainder the landfall area. Near shores and beaches try to locate marks every 200-500 yards with increasing distance between inland marks up to a mark along the transect until the marks edge of highwater.

   c. River sections –Once the transects have been flagged, focus on moving inland along rivers and streams. For very wide water bodies, flag marks on both shores. Emphasize flagging marks near bridges and constrictions or at breaks in stream slopes with multiple marks leading up to, under, and away from the bridge so that still water and drawdown conditions are documented.

   d. The best marks are found inside closed structures, or other places that are sheltered from wave action. Always try to find other marks nearby that will corroborate with the one you found.

   b. Documenting marks

      (1) Location - Note the mark's location on the map and in the field notes. Identify the transect, quad map, street address, and latitude and longitude, if available, in the field notes. Notes should be taken of the location of the mark in or on the structure, and a sketch should be made. Detailed descriptions should be made so that another person could find the mark using the notes. An identifying mark should be made with chalk, magic marker, paint, flagging, etc. in case the actual mark is destroyed by cleaning or rain. The mark should also be assigned a number which is noted at

the site, in the notes, and on the map. Preliminary measurements from the floor or ground to the mark should be made using a steel tape or engineer's rule.

(2) Classification – Based on circumstances and physical evidence determine whether the mark is the result of wave action, still-water surge, or riverine flooding and so indicate on the field form. The notes should also indicate whether the mark is inside or outside of a structure.

(3) Characterization -The mark should be classified by line type, such as debris, seed, stain, wash, drift, etc. The quality of the line should also be noted as a function of the spread or scatter of highwater mark material and the continuity of the mark: Excellent +/1 .05 ft., Good +/- 0.1 ft., Fair +/- 0.25 ft., Poor > 0.25 ft.

(3) Photographs - At least one photo should be taken of each high-water mark. Because the lines defining high-water marks can often be faint, the line should be pointed to or otherwise marked for ease in identification in the photo. A photo of the structure should also be taken to facilitate finding it again at a later date. Keep a log of photos taken.

(4) Other - For each high-water mark, identify the members of the flagging crew, the day, and the time of day.

4. Surveying high-water marks -Deferential surveying

a. Peg test - Conduct a 2-peg test once a week. Note the serial number of the level, the type of rod used, the persons conducting the test, and the date.

b. Survey procedures – In general, follow survey standards for indirect flow determinations as described by USGS TWRI Book 3, Chapter A1 (http://pubs.usgs.gov/twri/twri3-a1/html/pdf/twri_3-A1_a.pdf). Run a survey loop from a temporary benchmark (TBM) to each high-water mark using standard surveying rules for accuracy (+/- 0.01 ft for highwater marks). Make at least one ground shot for a representative ground elevation and one water-surface shot for a representative water-surface elevation (if possible). Also survey the tops of levees or roads and ground surfaces on each side. Note the TBM identification, high-water mark number, transect, surveying crew, date, and time of day. Keep standard surveying notes.

c. Sketches - Make a detailed sketch or sketches showing location of bench mark, high-water marks, presence of bridges, dunes, etc., and approximate surveying route.

d. Maps - Transfer the high-water mark elevations to maps and note similarity to elevations of nearby marks. If elevations differ significantly, try to find out why.

III. WATER QUALITY DATA COLLECTION

A. Manpower - The WSC Water-Quality Specialist is responsible for organizing the collection of water quality data from areas impacted by the storm. Crews should be made up of two persons each, one to drive the boat, and another to collect samples and conduct measurements. The number of crews used will depend on the size of the impacted area, the sampling coverage desired, and funding.

B. Equipment - Each crew will require a vehicle, boat, sample bottles, Hydrolab, maps, and field notebook. A camera should also be used to record significant effects of the storm, such as damaged trees and fishkills.

C. Sampling Parameters - Dissolved oxygen and biochemical oxygen demand are the important parameters to measure immediately after the storm's passage, especially in wetlands. Nutrient information is also desirable to further document the effects of the storm. Chloride concentration, or specific conductance, is good indicators of the extent of salt-water intrusion into freshwater areas.

D. Sampling frequency - The number of sites sampled is dependent on the availability of funds, the size of the area covered, and the level of coverage desired. The sites should be resampled at a rate sufficient to determine the storm's impact on water quality and the recovery of water quality to normal conditions. The resampling rate will often be higher during the first weeks after the storm, then slow down later as recovery rates are determined.

APPENDIX F
CIVIL AIR PATROL FORMS

Civil Air Patrol (CAP) over flight support	
Name of requester:	\<your name\>
Agency:	\<your office goes here\>
Office location:	\<please give city, state\>
Telephone:	\<best way(s) to reach you\>
Fax:	\<your local office/ICP fax goes here\>
Email:	\<your e-mail\>
Significant weather/event type:	\<some options are: coastal pre-storm assessment; hurricanes; severe convective outbreaks, including tornadoes, hail, and high winds; wildfires; tsunamis; river flooding; winter storms; volcanic eruptions; long term inland flooding, long term ice movement, etc.\>
Date of occurrence of event:	\<when will or did this event occur?\>
Time of occurrence of event:	\<when will or did this event occur?\>
state(s):	\<where will or did this event occur?\>
County(ies):	\<where will or did this event occur?\>
nearest populated area(s):	\<where will or did this event occur?\>

Location and description of flight support required \<attach simple map showing flight route\>

state(s) of flight:	\<location of flight\>
County(ies) of flight:	\<location of flight\>
nearest population area(s):	\<location of flight\>

Identify action to be taken on flight: \<Flight only, photography\>

estimated flight time:	
estimated flight distance:	

Any other information (e.g., additional contacts, additional Federal passengers):
If flight could prevent loss of life and/or property explain that here in detail.

E-mail to:nws.ofcm.cap@noaa.gov (subject = "CAP Request") or fax to 301-427-2007; then call 301-427-2002.

Post Civil Air Patrol (CAP) Flight Form	
Month/Date/Year of CAP flight:	<mm/dd/yy>
Type of aircraft utilized:	<Type of CAP aircraft used during mission>
Location of CAP flight:	<general description of where flight took place>
Total Flight Hours:	<CAP crew can provide this info>
CAP cost (if known):	<CAP crew might be able to provide this info>
Office(s) affected:	<list local offices participating on flight>
Personnel onboard:	<list local office personnel onboard with job title>
What was learned from this overflight mission/other pertinent details:	<some options are: final EF-scale rating; if other federal passengers were onboard; any direct benefit(s) from doing overflight (vs. a ground survey); key insights for damage assessment or coastal pre-storm assessment; etc.>

Upon completion of the mission utilizing CAP, and no later than 14 days after, e-mail this completed form to nws.ofcm.cap@noaa.gov (with subject = *"CAP mission report"*).

If this was a *NWS mission*, e-mail to: nws.metwatch@noaa.gov (with subject = *"CAP mission report"*)

*** OFCM is the federal lead for tracking, coordinating and reimbursing CAP flight costs.

APPENDIX G
PRE-SCRIPTED MISSION ASSIGNMENT

MISSION ASSIGNMENT PROPOSED STATEMENT 0F WORK (PSOW)		
Federal Department/Agency:	**ESF #:** **Supporting Mitigation Operations**	**Tracking No.:**
I. Title:		**Date:** MM-DD-YYYY
II. Description of Requested Assistance		
IV. Justification/Statement of Work		
IV. Cost Estimate: **Total Estimated Cost: TBD**		

FEMA COORDINATION					
Organization	**Date**	**Approve/Disapprove**	**Organization**	**Date**	**Approve/Disapprove**
Response Div.			OCC		
Recovery/PA Div.			CFO		
Logistics					
Mitigation					

Disaster Impact Assessments and Plans (DIAP) Statement of Work
For
Potential Pre-Scripted Mission Assignment

Federal Agencies: US Army Corps of Engineers (USACE), National Oceanographic and Atmospheric Administration (NOAA) and the United States Geological Survey (USGS)

Title: Collection of Storm Surge Water Level, High Water Mark, and Real-time Overland Wind Data

I Introduction

The purpose of this Mission Assignment is to enhance the capabilities of ESF #5, 9 and 14 coordinators with real time data to be used in a pre- and post disaster environment. Real time data will enable **Emergency Management, ESF #5**, coordinators to significantly augment emergency management operations by providing accurate and reliable scenarios for life safety operations and Incident Management decision making. **Urban Search & Rescue, ESF #9,** coordinators and **Hazard Performance and Analysis Teams** will be able to use the information to delineate damage areas to better organize their reconnaissance. This will enable the teams to respond with the appropriate technical members for each area to be investigated. Finally, **Long Term Community Recovery, ESF #14,** coordinators can begin to work with community officials to re-enact the event and offer accurate planning mitigation practices. The immediate use of this and other data can support critical re-entry planning or response decision making as well as to support **HMGP**, **NFIP** and other FEMA programs. This data can be analyzed to show the findings and trends.

The Office of Federal Coordinator for Meteorological Service and Supporting Research has established the Working Group for Disaster Impact Assessments and Plans: Weather and Water Data (WG/DIAP) to ensure a coordinated effort to collect environmental data that is imperative to properly monitor and characterize storms and floods. The Working Group consists of elements from NOAA, USACE, USGS, and FEMA and affiliated participants. A detailed data-collection plan is available at http://www.ofcm.gov/homepage/text/pubs.htm. In general, this plan outlines the process to deploy new technologies that transmit real-time reporting of some water elevations and wind data. This Mission Assignment tasks the WG/DIAP, through its constituent agencies, to accomplish the specific elements of the plan that support FEMA response and recovery operations under Section 402(3) of the Amended Stafford Act.

II Description of Requested Assistance

This PSMA tasks:

(1) The USGS with pre-positioning telemetered and non-telemetered sensors to record stream, river, and overland flood depths and the USACE for the pre-positioning of similar equipment to record near shore depths and wave heights during storm-induced flooding, especially storm surge;

(2) NOAA with pre-positioning multiple, portable overland weather monitoring stations to record vital wind speed, wind direction, temperature, and barometric pressure data, and relay this data in real-time to NOAA and emergency managers;

(3) USGS, NOAA, and USACE for support of FEMA and FEMA contractors for the post-storm acquisition and analysis of high water mark and wind data

III Justification

The purpose of the above three tasks is to facilitate an improvement in forecasting, disaster management, and recovery activities by the deployment of real-time and post-storm monitoring equipment (wind, surge and flood data) in the path of the storm prior to landfall and to expedite the computation of advisory flood elevations and claims settlements by gathering high water mark and wind data. These data can also be used by Hazard Performance and Analysis Teams to rapidly quantify damage in support of disaster assessment.

Emergency managers depend greatly on wind and river data for planning and managing hurricane and flood-disaster response and recovery operations. But often, there are too few hardened stations to adequately monitor wind and flood conditions to support operations before, during, or after a disaster.

In recent years the USGS, NOAA, USACE, and university researchers have developed mobile wind and water sensors that can be rapidly deployed to monitor hurricane impacts along the coast and inland. While these sensors were originally developed for research, some can provide real-time data that can be used by forecasters and emergency planners to assess pending damages and monitor evacuation routes and potential staging areas.

IV Statement of Work

(1) The USGS will deploy mobile sensors to form a network that will transmit tidal surge or inland water elevation data as frequently as every 15 minutes. These sensors will be strapped to selected bridge piers, power poles and fire hydrants at approximately 30-70 locations along the coast, in rivers, or in low lying areas. While most instruments will provide data for post-storm purposes, selected units will provide real time data. These real-time units will be placed along hurricane evacuation routes, near important infrastructure (roads, bridges, water and waste-water facilities, hospitals), and at other potential response-recovery staging facilities. This will provide emergency managers with reconnaissance level information about the storm's maximum and current water depths and the associated rates of rise and fall. This real-time data will allow response teams to rapidly assess the pending disaster area for staging areas and to estimate the duration of flooding at pre-determined critical facilities or shelters. Following the storm, the USGS will recover the instruments and download the data for the non-telemetered sites and place it on a USGS webpage (Waterdata.usgs.gov/XX/nwis/rt where "XX" is the 2-letter abbreviation for the state of interest). The USGS will also survey all of the instruments to a common elevation datum so that the data can be used to aide in the development of a flood map. A detailed work plan is available at http://www.ofcm.gov/homepage/text/pubs.htm.

(2) NOAA has contracted with the Digital Hurricane Consortium, headed by the University of Florida to pre-position portable weather monitoring stations to record vital wind speed, wind direction, temperature, and barometric pressure data in and around the area of hurricane landfall. This data will then be relayed in real-time to NOAA monitoring stations consisting of 6 trailer mounted instrument towers that can be deployed and set up prior to landfall. Typically, several towers are clustered near the area of projected landfall, while others are spread along the coast. This provides a recording of both the peak and the breadth of intensity. The specific deployment strategy can be altered within hours of landfall to optimize the dataset, which is a function of specific storm parameters (size, intensity, translation speed). Instrument deployment teams have historically worked closely with NOAA HRD personnel to jointly plan deployments. The program has been operational since 1999, and has been providing real-time data streams since Isabel in 2003. The real-time data stream has been used by HRD to refine intensity forecasting just prior to landfall (example: Dennis, 2005).

(3) USGS and USACE will support FEMA and FEMA contractors by deploying personnel to flooded areas to identify, characterize, and denote high water locations. In addition, if requested by FEMA, they will survey the high water marks to a common datum. At its own expense, the USGS will determine the high water elevations and report the magnitude of flood flows at current USGS stream gauges and will attempt to assign a recurrence interval to those flows. If FEMA tasks them, the USGS will also flag high water marks at discontinued stream gauges, flood-peak gauging stations, and other locations of significant interests (bridges, dams, etc.). If hydraulic conditions are favorable, the USGS will determine peak flows to aide in assigning a recurrence interval to the flood flows at these locations. USGS and USACE operations for denoting high water mark locations and the subsequent surveying will be performed in a manner consistent with FEMA protocols, except at stream gauging stations and flood-peak gauging stations where high water marks, river profiles, and stream cross-sections will be surveyed to more stringent USGS protocols to permit the computation of flows.

APPENDIX H
FEMA NATIONAL RESPONSE COORDINATION CENTER CRITICAL PHONE NUMBERS

AREA A

Position	Phone 202-646-xxxx	E-mail
FEMA NRCC Activation Team Box	n/a	FEMA-NRCC-activationteam@dhs.gov
DOD-NGB Liaison	2438	FEMA-NRCC-dodngb@dhs.gov
DOD Liaison	2438	FEMA-NRCC-dod@dhs.gov
DHS HSIN Liaison	2460	FEMA-NRCC-hsin@dhs.gov
NRCC Activation Team Officer	2425*	FEMA-NRCC-teamofficer@dhs.gov
NRCC Deputy Team Officer	2496	FEMA-NRCC-teamdeputy@dhs.gov
ESF 1	2441	FEMA-NRCC-esf01@dhs.gov
ESF 1 a	2441	FEMA-NRCC-esf01a@dhs.gov
Admin Specialist Leader	2424 / 2425*	FEMA-NRCC-adminlead@dhs.gov
Admin Assistant Specialist	2428	FEMA-NRCC-adminasst@dhs.gov
External Affairs PAO	2456	FEMA-NRCC-esf15pao@dhs.gov
External Affairs CLO	2457	FEMA-NRCC-esf15clo@dhs.gov
ESF 13	2490	FEMA-NRCC-esf13@dhs.gov
Security Specialist	2465	FEMA-NRCC-security@dhs.gov
Infrastructure Branch Director	3324	FEMA-NRCC-infradirector@dhs.gov
ESF 12	3201	FEMA-NRCC-esf12@dhs.gov
Logistics TAV Liaison	2435	FEMA-NRCC-logtav@dhs.gov
Logistics Support Deputy	2440	FEMA-NRCClogsupportdeputy@dhs.gov
Logistics Section Chief	2405	FEMA-NRCC-logsecchief@dhs.gov
ESF 8 a	2993	FEMA-NRCC-esf08a@dhs.gov
ESF 8 b	2468	FEMA-NRCC-esf08b@dhs.gov
ESF 8	2448	FEMA-NRCC-esf08@dhs.gov
Emergency Services Branch Director	2444	FEMA-NRCC-emdirector@dhs.gov
ESF 3 b	2762	FEMA-NRCC-esf03b@dhs.gov
ESF 3 a	2459	FEMA-NRCC-esf03a@dhs.gov
ESF 3	2443	FEMA-NRCC-esf03@dhs.gov
ESF 7 (GSA)	3382	FEMA-NRCC-esf07@dhs.gov
ESF 7 b (Liaison to LRC)	2429	FEMA-NRCC-esf07b@dhs.gov
ESF 11 a	2451	FEMA-NRCC-esf11a@dhs.gov
ESF 11	2413	FEMA-NRCC-esf11@dhs.gov

Area A (Continued)

Position	Phone 202-646-xxxx	E-mail
ESF 10 (EPA)	2466*	FEMA-NRCC-esf10epa@dhs.gov
ESF 10 (USCG)	2466*	FEMA-NRCC-esf10uscg@dhs.gov
ESF 4	2458*	FEMA-NRCC-esf04@dhs.gov
ESF 4 a	2458*	FEMA-NRCC-esf04a@dhs.gov
ESF 2	2442	FEMA-NRCC-esf02@dhs.gov
US Coast Guard Liaison	2431	FEMA-NRCC-uscg@dhs.gov
ESF 1 (Aviation)	3200	FEMA-NRCC-esf01avia@dhs.gov
Operations Deputy	2461	FEMA-NRCC-opsdeputy@dhs.gov
Operations Section Chief	2430	FEMA-NRCC-opschief@dhs.gov
ESF 14	2518	FEMA-NRCC-esf14@dhs.gov
Mitigation Planner	2467	FEMA-NRCC-mitigation@dhs.gov
Mitigation Planner b	2454	FEMA-NRCC-mitigationb@dhs.gov
F/A Admin Specialist	2420	FEMA-NRCC-financeadmin@dhs.gov
Donations Specialist	2453	FEMA-NRCC-donations@dhs.gov
NOVAD Specialist	2452	FEMA-NRCC-novad@dhs.gov
ESF 6 (Disaster Assistance Directorate)	2450	FEMA-NRCC-esf06@dhs.gov
Red Cross	2446	FEMA-NRCC-redcross@dhs.gov
Human Services Branch Director	2988	FEMA-NRCC-humsdirector@dhs.gov
Mission Assignment Coordinator	2464	FEMA-NRCC-mac@dhs.gov
Operations Action Tracker	2437	FEMA-NRCC-opsacttracker@dhs.gov
F/A Section Chief (Comptroller)	2491	FEMA-NRCC-comptroller@dhs.gov
F/A Financial Specialist	2476	FEMA-NRCC-financespec@dhs.gov
ESF 9 SAR Team Leader	2449	FEMA-NRCC-esf09sar@dhs.gov
ESF 9 Ops Specialist	2492	FEMA-NRCC-esf09ops@dhs.gov
ESF 9 Admin Specialist	2483	FEMA-NRCC-esf09admin@dhs.gov
FEMA Logistics Response Center (LRC)	**3226**	**FEMA-LRC-Chief@dhs.gov**

AREA B

Position	Phone 202-646-xxxx	e-mail
NRCC Watch Officer	2828	FEMA-NRCC@dhs.gov
Current Ops Plans Leader	2439*	FEMA-NRCC-curopsplan@dhs.gov
Planning Section Chief	2470*	FEMA-NRCC-planchief@dhs.gov
Deputy Planning Chief	2470*	FEMA-NRCC-plandeputy@dhs.gov
Current Ops Planner a	4512	FEMA-NRCC-curopsplan@dhs.gov
Current Ops Planner b	4580	FEMA-NRCC-curopsplan@dhs.gov
Current Ops Planner c	4560	FEMA-NRCC-curopsplan@dhs.gov
Current Ops Planner d	4551	FEMA-NRCC-curopsplan@dhs.gov
Documentation Reports Specialist	3476	FEMA-NRCC-docrpts@dhs.gov
NRCC Assistant Can answer 2470 / 2439*	2992	FEMA-NRCC-assistant@dhs.gov
Situation Status Unit Leader	2473	FEMA-NRCC-sitstatlead@dhs.gov
Situation Status Information Specialist a	2474*	FEMA-NRCC-sitstatinfoa@dhs.gov
Situation Status Information Specialist b	2474*	FEMA-NRCC-sitstatinfob@dhs.gov
NRCC Watch Analyst a (24/7)	2482	FEMA-NRCC@dhs.gov
NRCC Watch Analyst b (24/7)	2481	FEMA-NRCC@dhs.gov
NRCC Watch Analyst c (24/7)	2472	FEMA-NRCC@dhs.gov
NRCC Watch Analyst d (24/7)	3244	FEMA-NRCC@dhs.gov
Resource Tracking Specialist (LRC supports)	hold	FEMA-NRCC-restracking@dhs.gov
NOAA Liaison	2479	FEMA-NRCC-NOAAlno@dhs.gov
Resource Unit Leader	3248	FEMA-NRCC-reslead@dhs.gov
Documentation Unit Leader	2473	FEMA-NRCC-doclead@dhs.gov
VIP Briefing Specialist	3003	FEMA-NRCC-vipbriefer@dhs.gov
Situation Status Information Specialist c	2477	FEMA-NRCC-sitstatinfoc@dhs.gov
Situation Status Information Specialist d	2485	FEMA-NRCC-sitstatinfod@dhs.gov
Situation Status Information Specialist e	2463	FEMA-NRCC-sitstatinfoe@dhs.gov
CONOPS OMT Coordinator	2460	FEMA-NRCC-conops@dhs.gov
VACANT	4520	n/a
Pat Pritchett	3411	n/a
ESF 09 reports Specialist	2489	FEMA-NRCC-09reports@dhs.gov
Safety	2480	FEMA-NRCC-safety@dhs.gov
Secret Service Liaison	2413	FEMA-NRCC-secretsvc@dhs.gov
GIS Coordinator	2486	FEMA-NRCC-giscoord@dhs.gov
NOC Liaison	2747	FEMA-NRCC-NOClno@dhs.gov
Movement Coordination Branch	2989	FEMA-NRCC-mcb@dhs.gov
HR Admin	2747	FEMA-NRCC-hradmin@dhs.gov

Area B (Continued)

Position	Phone 202-646-xxxx	e-mail
TSA Liaison	2495	FEMA-NRCC-tsa@dhs.gov
EMAC State Support	2547	FEMA-NRCC-emacstate@dhs.gov
EMAC NGB	2547	FEMA-NRCC-emacngb@dhs.gov
DHS-IP Liaison (Infrastructure Protection)	2423	FEMA-NRCC-dhsiplno@dhs.gov
VACANT	2462	n/a
Remote Sensing (Technical Specialist)	2556	FEMA-NRCC-remotesensing@dhs.gov
MERS (Not a manned station – virtual contact)	n/a	FEMA-NRCC-mers@dhs.gov

APPENDIX I
DATA ACCESS

Consolidated Storm Event Data

Storm event data and metadata collected for individual storm events and shared by participants is compiled and made available by OFCM on the WG/DIAP web page:

http://www.ofcm.noaa.gov/wg-diap/metadata.htm.

Agency and Entity Data Disposition

Department of Agriculture (USDA)

All climate data collected by the NRCS can be accessed via the NRCS National Water and Climate Center (NWCC) website: http://www.wcc.nrcs.usda.gov.

Department of Commerce (DOC)

National Weather Service (NWS)

The NWS stores storm event data at: http://www.weather.gov/om/data/stormdata.shtml. Additional information on severe storm events can be accessed in NWS' Storm Data program at: http://www4.ncdc.noaa.gov/cgi-win/wwcgi.dll?wwEvent~Storms.

Imagery and other data captured during CAP missions will be stored by the agency requesting CAP support. Some of the data captured during 53 WRS missions is made available at: http://www.nhc.noaa.gov/reconlist.shtml.

National Ocean Service (NOS)

Center for Operational Oceanographic Products and Services (CO-OPS)

Under Development

Coastal Services Center (CSC)

CSC archives maps and products in the Charleston, SC office and sends them via FTP to DHS/FEMA and NOAA ICC during events.

Office of Response and Restoration (OR&R)

Under Development

National Geodetic Survey (NGS)

NGS data are initially stored at NOAA headquarters located in Silver Spring, MD, with a mirrored RAID site in Norfolk, VA. The imagery data are freely available to the public in JPEG format via the internet. These images were made available to emergency personnel and the public on the NOAA/NGS web site (http://www.ngs.noaa.gov/).

National Institute of Standards and Technology (NIST)

Personnel at the Building and Fire Research Laboratory at NIST investigate the performance of infrastructure after hazard events and produce reconnaissance reports which can be found at: http://www.bfrl.nist.gov/investigations/investigations.htm.

Department of Defense (DOD)

U.S. Army Corps of Engineers (USACE)

The USACE NCMP lidar data are available online through the NOAA Coastal Services Center Lidar Data Retrieval Tool at http://maps.csc.noaa.gov/TCM/. For all other USACE data please contact the USACE personnel listed in the WG/DIAP contact information list located on the WG/DIAP web page: http://www.ofcm.gov/wg-diap/index.htm

Department of Homeland Security (DHS)

Federal Emergency Management Agency (FEMA)

Under Development

Department of the Interior (DOI)

U.S. Geological Survey (USGS)

Various USGS data are stored in different locations depending of the type of data, frequency of recordings, and length of the data record.

Streamflow monitoring – Real-time water-level and flow data for about 6,800 streamgages are available at http://waterdata.usgs.gov/nwis/rt. Interactive maps of the current National and state level flow conditions (relative to flooding or drought) are available at http://water.usgs.gov/waterwatch/. Maps and tables summarizing recent flooding conditions are available at http://water.usgs.gov/cgi-bin/wwdp.

Flood measurements –Summaries of recent flood measurements (width, depth, velocities, etc.) are distributed at http://waterdata.usgs.gov/nwis/measurements for each state and streamgage.

Flood forensics –Indirect flow measurements are computed and summarized in non-published reports that may be viewed at the relevant USGS state office. Contract information for these state offices is available at http://water.usgs.gov/district_chief.html.

Storm-tide monitoring -. Real-time storm-surge data (for periods during and immediately after the storm) can be viewed by accessing storm-surge sites listed in state streamflow summary tables (http://waterdata.usgs.gov/XX/nwis/rt) where "XX" refers to the 2-letter abbreviation for the state of interest. As data are corrected and finalized, they are published in online "data series" reports with ASCII tab-delimited or fix-column format at http://water.usgs.gov/osw/programs/storm_surge.html.

Rapid-Deployable Gages –These data are available at http://waterdata.usgs.gov/XX/nwis/rt where "XX" refers to the 2-letter abbreviation for the state of interest.

Flood documentation – When the data are used by the USGS to construct flood maps, the data are available through USGS publications at http://pubs.er.usgs.gov/usgspubs/recentpubs.jsp.

Shoreline Change - State-of-the art research vessels, Global Positioning System (GPS) satellites, and side-scan survey and velocity measurement equipment are used to collect post-storm data. Images and data are available at http://coastal.er.usgs.gov/shoreline-change/.

Department of the Transportation (DOT)

The Federal Highway Administration (FHWA)

The FHWA, though not a current participant, is expected to become more involved in the future. While they have no requirements to acquire environmental data following significant storm events, they work with state and local DOTs who are building the capabilities to do so. These sites, which monitor the highway system, could eventually be used in the storm event data acquisition process.

American Association for Wind Engineering (AAWE)

If AAWE members collect storm event data through a coordinated AAWE deployment, AAWE will retain a copy of data collected. AAWE may be contacted to arrange data transfer at the following URL www.aawe.org, and email aawe@aawe.org.

Coasts, Oceans, Ports and Rivers Institute (COPRI)

Under Development

Digital Hurricane Consortium (DHC)

The Digital Hurricane Consortium stores storm event data (field measurements of land falling hurricane wind data as well as metadata) in the following locations: http://fcmp.ce.ufl.edu/, http://www.atmo.ttu.edu/TTUHRT/, and http://www.digitalhurricane.org/.

APPENDIX J
ABBREVIATIONS AND ACRONYMS

-A-

AAWE	American Association for Wind Engineering
AOC	[NMAO] Aircraft Operations Center
ASP	Aeronautical Survey Program [of NOAA/NGS]

-C-

CAMEO	Computer Aided Management to Emergency Operations
CAP	Civil Air Patrol
CMP	[NOAA/NGS] Coastal Mapping Program
CO-OPS	Center for Operational Oceanic Products and Services
COPRI	Coasts, Oceans, Ports and Rivers Institute
CSC	Coastal Services Center
CSWR	Center for Severe Weather Research

-D-

DHC	Digital Hurricane Consortium
DHS	Department of Homeland Security
DOC	Department of Commerce
DOD	Department of Defense
DOI	Department of Interior
DOT	Department of Transportation

-E-

EF	Enhanced Fujita [Tornado Intensity Scale]
ERDC	Engineering Research and Development Center
EROS	[USGS] Earth Resources Observation and Science [Center]
ESF	Emergency Support Function [of the National Response Framework]

-F-

FCO	[FEMA] Federal Coordinating Officer
FEMA	Federal Emergency Management Agency
FHWA	Federal Highway Administration

-G-

GD	Geologic Division
GIS	geographic information system
GPS	Global Positioning System
GSD	ground sample distance

-H-

HAZMAT	hazardous materials
HSOC	[NOAA] Homeland Security Operations Center

-I-

IAA	Inter-Agency Agreement
ICC	[NOAA] Incident Coordination Center

-J-

JFO   [FEMA] Joint Field Office

-M-

MAT   [FEMA] Mitigation Assessment Team

-N-

NCEP   National Centers for Environmental Prediction
NCMP   [USACE] National Coastal Mapping Program
NESDIS   National Environmental Satellite, Data, and Information Service
NGS   National Geodetic Survey
NIST   National Institute of Standards and Technology
NMAO   NOAA Marine and Aviation Operations
NOAA   National Oceanic and Atmospheric Administration
NOS   National Ocean Service
NPDIA   National Plan for Disaster Impact Assessments: Weather and Water Data
NRCC   National Response Coordination Center
NRCS   Natural Resources Conservation Service
NWS   National Weather Service

-O-

OAR   [NOAA] Office of Oceanic and Atmospheric Research
OCWWS   Office of Climate, Water, and Weather Services
OFCM   Office of the Federal Coordinator for Meteorological Services and Supporting
                          Research
OR&R   Office of Response and Restoration

-Q-

QRT   Quick Response Team

-S-

SCAN   Soil Climate Analysis Network
SLOSH   Sea, Lake, and Overland Surges from Hurricanes [computer model]
SNOTEL   SNOw TELemtry
SPC   Storm Prediction Center

-U-

URL   Uniform Resource Locator
USACE   United States Army Corps of Engineers
USAF   United States Air Force
USDA   United States Department of Agriculture
USGS   United States Geological Survey

-W-

WCM   Warning Coordination Meteorologist
WFO   [NWS] Weather Forecast Office
WG/DIAP   Working Group for Disaster Impact Assessments and Plans: Weather and Water Data
WRS   [USAF] Weather Reconnaissance Squadron

APPENDIX K
EXAMPLES OF PAST DISASTER IMPACT ASSESSMENTS

Hurricane Hugo

Hurricane Hugo made landfall on the United States mainland near Charleston, South Carolina, late on 21 September 1989. The U. S. Geological Survey (USGS) District Chief approached the USACE to cooperate in an aerial photoreconnaissance effort of the affected reach of shoreline. The National Oceanic and Atmospheric Administration's (NOAA) National Weather Service (NWS) performed an extensive review of its operations during the event. An informal agreement was reached whereby the USGS would assume responsibility for leveling water marks identified by both USACE and USGS field teams, and the USACE would assume responsibility for acquiring aerial photo reconnaissance in a format acceptable to both agencies.

Over 350 high-water marks were identified and leveled, and over 250 controlled aerial photos covering approximately 150 miles of coastline (from Little River Inlet to Edisto Island, South Carolina) were surveyed as a result of the ad hoc agreement between USACE and USGS. Subsequent to acquisition of these data, the Federal Emergency Management Agency (FEMA) partially reimbursed the USGS for its efforts. Both USGS and USACE published reports based upon the inundation data and aerial imagery. In an independent effort, the NWS performed an extensive review of its operations during the event and conducted a visual damage survey via aircraft.

Hurricane Andrew

Hurricane Andrew made first landfall on the continental United States near Homestead, Florida, early on the morning of 24 August 1992 and second landfall near Morgan City, Louisiana, on 26 August 1992. Three agencies were active in the Florida post-event survey; USACE, USGS, and the Florida Department of Natural Resources, a state agency.

As in Hugo, FEMA mission-assigned the USGS for the post-storm Andrew efforts. The USACE, primarily through the efforts of the Jacksonville District with assistance from the Waterways Experiment Station, performed extensive surveys of federal projects along the east and southwest coasts of Florida. The Florida Department of Natural Resources acquired low-level videotape imagery of the Florida east coast from Palm Beach to Key Biscayne and also performed some high-water surveys. All agencies published reports on their respective findings.

Hurricane Katrina

Hurricane Katrina destroyed or damaged extensive areas of coastal Louisiana, Mississippi, and parts of Alabama. Dozens of USGS, NOAA, and USACE river, tide gages, offshore buoys and meteorological observing systems were destroyed, many of which ceased reporting well before the storm crest. The loss of these systems hampered the assessment of flood, wind, and wave damage; complicated the forecasting of near-term flood and surge conditions; hindered the management of operations to dewater New Orleans; and frustrated the post-storm evaluation of levee performance and evaluation of coastal impacts due to waves and surge. As a result, the preservation of high-water mark data took on a heightened importance in the delineation of flood impact areas for insurance settlement, and the determination of advisory base flood elevations needed for reconstruction. In the aftermath of the storm, FEMA, USGS, and USACE collaborated on an extensive program to preserve high-water marks and map flood-impact areas but the efforts were not closely coordinated. While more than 1,000 high-water marks were eventually flagged and leveled, the work was undertaken in a patchwork process that evolved through personal contact and individual effort. As a result some data collection efforts were poorly integrated, delayed or incomplete and the quality of some of the data suffered because of miscommunications and inconsistent collection methods. Following this event, NOAA and the USGS began an effort to establish several hurricane-hardened coastal tide gauges on the Gulf Coast featuring a single-pile design built to withstand a major hurricane.

The lack of bathymetric survey data offshore of the MS mainland coast, MS Sound, and offshore of the MS barrier islands hindered post-storm studies to evaluate impacts and the evaluation of impacts due to potential future storms.

Research teams from the University of Florida and Texas Tech University deployed portable hardened wind observing stations prior to landfall, providing the only source of reliable high resolution overland ground level wind speed / direction data throughout the storm. Portions of this dataset were transmitted in real-time to the NWS and NOAA's Hurricane Research Division (HRD) to aid in intensity forecasts. Research teams coordinated with NOAA for placement of the portable systems. The teams on the ground retrieved immediately perishable structural performance data in the process of retrieving the equipment. Overland ground level wind measurement assets have been deployed in this manner since 1999 through university wind research programs, including deployment in over 20 hurricanes and tropical storms.

Midwest Flooding

Flooding occurred on numerous Midwestern rivers during 2008. Indiana experienced the most recurrent flooding during 2008, with record floods occurring during the months of January, February, March, June, and September. The Midwestern June floods were by far the most severe and widespread with record flooding and damage occurring in Illinois, Indiana, Iowa, Missouri, and Wisconsin. USGS cooperated with numerous local, state, and Federal agencies to collect flood data both during and after these flood events.

Formal flood documentation studies and reports were produced for the June 2008 flooding in parts of Indiana and Wisconsin through an interagency agreement with FEMA Region 5. These studies included high water profiles and inundation mapping. The USGS also flagged high water marks and did limited surveys of these marks in numerous other locations in Iowa, Illinois, Missouri, and Arkansas for various floods during 2008. A USGS fact sheet was produced for the Arkansas flooding in March and April 2008 with funding provided from the U.S. Army Corps of Engineers. Two reports are being prepared to document high-water profiles for the June floods along the Upper Iowa, Iowa, and Cedar River Basins in Iowa with funding from the Iowa DOT; and an overall report is being prepared to document all significant flooding in Iowa in 2008. The USGS, through the International Charter, U.S. Air Force EagleVision, and Landsat, assisted in the acquisition of satellite imagery for Midwest flood areas over the course of 2008. Flood documentation reports for the 2008 flooding have or are being published by other agencies on their respective findings.

APPENDIX L
WORKING GROUP FOR DISASTER IMPACT ASSESSMENTS AND PLANS: WEATHER AND WATER DATA

Chairman
Mr. Robert Mason
U.S. Geological Survey
Water Resources Discipline

Executive Secretary
Mr. Anthony Ramirez
Office of the Federal Coordinator for
    Meteorological Services and Supporting
    Research

Department of Agriculture
Ms. Claudia Hoeft, P.E.
Snow Survey and Water Supply Forecasting
Conservation Engineering Division
Natural Resources Conservation Service

Mr. Noller Herbert
Director, Conservation Engineering
    Division,
Natural Resources Conservation Service

Department of Commerce
National Oceanic and Atmospheric
Administration (NOAA)
Ms. Allison L. Allen
CO-OPS
National Ocean Service

Mr. Michael L. Aslaksen, Jr.
Chief, Remote Sensing Division
National Ocean Service

Mr. Eric Berkowitz
Deputy Chief, Remote Sensing Division
National Ocean Service

Mr. Todd Davison
Coastal Services Center
National Ocean Service

Mr. Michael Lowry
National Hurricane Center
National Centers for Environmental
    Prediction
National Weather Service

NOAA (Continued)
Mr. Chris Maier
National Weather Service

Mr. Doug Marcy
Coastal Services Center
National Ocean Service

Dr. Wilson A. Shaffer
Office of Science and Technology
Meteorological Development Laboratory
National Weather Service

Department of Commerce
National Institute of Standards and
Technology (NIST)
Mr. Eric Letvin
Disaster and Failures Study Program
Engineering Laboratory

Dr. Long T. Phan
Materials and Construction Research
    Division

Department of Defense
U.S. Army Corps of Engineers
(USACE)
Mr. William (Bill) Birkemeier
Supervisory Research Hydraulic Engineer
US Army Engineer Research and
Development Center
Coastal and Hydrologic Laboratory

Mr. Jeffrey D. Jensen
Institute for Water Resources

USACE (Continued)

Ms. Linda S. Lillycrop
US Army Engineer Research and
Development Center
Coastal and Hydraulics Laboratory
Navigation Division
Coastal Engineering Branch

Mr. Michael Schuster
Baltimore District, AICP

Department of Homeland Security
Mr. Dan Catlett
Hurricane Preparedness Program
Federal Emergency Management Agency

Dr. Richard D. Jacques
National Operations Center

Mr. Seth Spoelman
Federal Emergency Management Agency

Mr. Alan Springett
Federal Emergency Management Agency
Region II, Mitigation

Mr. Paul Tertell
Federal Emergency Management Agency

Department of the Interior
U.S. Geological Survey (USGS)
Dr. Robert R. Holmes
USGS National Flood Coordinator
Office of Surface Water

Mr. D. Phil Turnipseed
Hydrologist
Office of Surface Water

Department of Transportation
Federal Highway Administration
(FHWA)
Mr. Paul A. Pisano
Road Weather Program
Office of Operations

Affiliated Organizations

American Association for Wind Engineering (AAWE)
Dr. Leighton Cochran
Senior Associate
Cermak Peterka Petersen Inc

Dr. Kurt Gurley
Structures Group
Department of Civil and Coastal
Engineering
University of Florida

Dr. Nicholas P. Jones
President, AAWE
Benjamin T. Rome Dean, Whiting School of
Engineering
Johns Hopkins University

Dr. Forrest Masters
Department of Civil & Coastal Engineering
University of Florida

Coasts, Oceans, Ports, and Rivers Institute (COPRI)
Dr. Billy L. Edge
Program Head, Sustainable Coastal
Engineering
UNC Coastal Studies Institute
Professor, Civil, Construction, and
Environmental Engineering Dept.
North Carolina State University

Digital Hurricane Consortium (DHC)
Mr. Bill Coulbourne, P.E.
Director, Wind & Flood Hazard Mitigation
Applied Technology Council (ATC)

DHC (Continued)

Dr. Kurt Gurley
Structures Group
Department of Civil and Coastal
    Engineering
University of Florida

Andrew Kennedy
Department of Civil Engineering and
Geological Sciences
University of Notre Dame

Dr. Forrest Masters
Department of Civil & Coastal Engineering
University of Florida

Other Participants and Observers

Mr. Lee W. Aggers
USGS

Mr. Eric Berman
Department of Homeland Security
Federal Emergency Management Agency

Ms. Sherry Durst
USGS
U.S. Northern Command

Dr. Andrew Garcia
U.S. Army Corps of Engineers (retired)

Mr. Al Mongeon
NOAA Meteorologist
NWS Homeland Security Activities

Dr. Gavin Smith
DHS Center of Excellence—Natural
    Disasters, Coastal Infrastructure and
    Emergency Management

Mr. Regis Walters
NOAA Homeland Security Program Office
National Ocean Service

**Other Participants and Observers
(Continued)**

Mr. Don Woodward
(Retired) NRCS National Hydraulic
    Engineer
U.S. Department of Agriculture